Secrets of
Spiritual Happiness

❧

In *Never to Return*, Sharon Janis shared intimate, humorous, and profound moments from her colorful spiritual journey...Publishers Weekly said in their review: "In a larger sense, this memoir is a dialogue between Indian spirituality and Western psychology. The question that Janis answers in her memoir is: 'Can a westerner come to know Indian spirituality and flourish in its depths, even when it is alien to western ways of knowing?' She answers with a resounding 'yes.'"

In *Spirituality for Dummies*, Sharon boiled down this elusive topic with humor and insight. The Village Voice wrote: "If you feel empty inside (and not because it's been six hours since your last burrito), it might be time to search for the meaning of life in Spirituality for Dummies...Even skeptics can gain self-knowledge from the thought and visualization exercises strewn throughout the book, which demonstrate how to take a positive view of negative experiences and let go of emotional baggage – like going to a therapist, but cheaper."

Now, Sharon Janis unravels the *Secrets of Spiritual Happiness*.

About the Author

Sharon Janis is a spiritual artist and philosopher who lived a decade of monastic life, then entered Hollywood as an editor and producer of several popular shows, including *Candid Camera, X-Men,* and the *Mighty Morphin' Power Rangers.* She currently works through Night Lotus Productions, and is the primary investigator on a study of bioethics funded by the National Institute of Mental Health.

Sharon, also known as her guru-given name Kumuda, is also the author of *Never to Return* and *Spirituality for Dummies.* She lives in Cardiff By The Sea, California.

Secrets of

Spiritual Happiness

ଔ

Sharon Janis

Cold Spring Press

COLD SPRING PRESS
P.O. Box 284, Cold Spring Harbor, NY 11724
E-mail: Jopenroad@aol.com

Library of Congress Control No. 2003104440
ISBN 1-892975-98-X

Printed in the United States of America

Table of Contents

May all be happy and contented.
May all be healthy and prosperous.
May all experience auspiciousness and goodness.
May no one face misfortune or sorrow.

– Universal Prayer

Introduction

"You are looking for happiness in the wrong places!" We've heard this in every scripture, in every new-age workshop, in every religious sermon, in every self-help seminar, and in just about every spiritual book. "You're looking for happiness in the wrong places! You're looking outside yourself; you have to look within. You're looking for enduring happiness in temporary pleasures instead of turning within to find the eternal wellspring of true satisfaction, fulfillment, and spiritual happiness inside yourself!" But what does it really mean to find happiness within?

Some find happiness in receiving, some in giving, some in accomplishing, and some in wealth, health, love, inner peace, respect, power, beauty, talents, or a loving and harmonious family life. You may experience happiness from your work, from physical sports, from lovemaking, from a restful evening, from exciting movies, from a good book, from every possible kind of music that you can imagine, or from achieving a particular goal that you've been earnestly working toward.

Nevertheless, even with so much to be happy about, many people are still unhappy, or not as happy as they would like to be. Well, get ready to put on your best smiling heart, because we're going to help remedy that right now, from the roots out.

The purpose of this book is to initiate you into a more expanded view of what it truly means to have happiness, and in particular, spiritual happiness.

Spiritual happiness is a deep contentment and joy that exists beneath all the superficial waves of ephemeral life. It is a faith and gratitude that never leaves you, flourishing throughout the ups and downs of life.

Preliminary Notes

Regarding Quotes:

In *Secrets of Spiritual Happiness* I have included a variety of relevant quotes from many sources and traditions to help unfold this vast and grand topic. In lieu of limiting these accomplished beings to just a several-word description of who they are and what they've done in their lives, I've chosen to simply give their names. If you are curious to find out more about a particular source, you can "google" them (search for their name on an internet search engine) to find more substantial biographies there.

Regarding Personal Relevance:

In this book, I share many personal stories and lessons. Please be aware that your life lessons may differ from mine, and that we're often growing into and through different lessons at different times. Therefore, if any of my interpretations of particular events don't ring true for you at this time in your life, then please trust your own inner guide above anything that you read – in this book or anywhere.

Regarding God:

"God" is one of many words that can be used to describe the great magnificence that is both known and unknown. In this book, I use the term "God" in its general sense, and not as described by any one religion or tradition. If the word "God" doesn't accurately represent your personal image and relationship, then please feel free to replace this word with any He, She, It, form, or formlessness that works for you.

Section One:
Exploring Happiness

Happiness is the meaning and the purpose of life, the whole aim and end of human existence.
—Aristotle

Everyone in this world desires happiness, although few know exactly what is meant by the word. How do you define happiness?

Some terms used to officially define the word happiness are: Favored by luck or fortune, enjoying a state of well-being and contentment, marked by an atmosphere of good fellowship, and a pleasurable or satisfying experience.

What do you feel when you are able to truthfully say that you are happy? What brings greater happiness into *your* life?

There isn't really a single answer to what brings happiness, although each of us can hopefully recall times when our hearts have sung with transcendent joy. We want to recreate those precious moments, and perhaps expand them into a state of steady happiness, and yet, as quickly as a sunset, we may find happiness slipping from our grasp, again and again.

According to an impressive number of spiritual philosophers, happiness is, in fact, our birthright. It is ours for the experiencing. Nevertheless, if we don't really know what true happiness is, or how to cultivate its sweet fragrance inside ourselves, then our efforts to find true happiness in outer circumstances alone are likely to be in vain.

The Science of Happiness

In medical circles, the experience of being happy can be ascribed to having a proper abundance of the chemical neurotransmitter serotonin in your brain. When the levels of serotonin in your brain are too low, you can be expected to also experience a decrease in a particular sense of subjective well-being that is generally described by the word "happiness." Many common anti-depressant medications work either by increasing the amount of serotonin in your brain, or by increasing your brain's receptivity to serotonin. However, having too much serotonin in your brain can also create feelings of sadness and unhappiness. Therefore, seeking refuge in "chemical happiness" alone can be quite a challenging balancing act in the long-term.

Other scientists have theorized that human beings have actually evolved to be dissatisfied, suggesting that early humans who were dissatisfied were apt to try a little harder to acquire the necessities and comforts of life. Perhaps this trait of dissatisfaction would inspire them to hunt a little better, to stash away more food, or to find a way to keep a bit warmer — practices that would have increased the likelihood of a longer life. With this longer life, came more opportunities for passing on their "dissatisfaction gene" for generations to come – and here we are.

Just think, the root of your present feelings of dissatisfaction may stem from the genetic DNA patterns of your "great, great, great, great, etc." grandpa, who wasn't content with having mere berries to eat, and was thus inspired by his dissatisfaction to take a course on *Hunting Buffalos 101*, or to figure out how to irrigate the fields, or to plant a greater variety of food sources.

With this "hereditary dissatisfaction" theory in mind, I'd like to suggest that even if you *do* feel dissatisfaction with certain elements in your life, this does not mean that you have to consider yourself to be "unhappy."

This is important to contemplate, because our experience of happiness is generally dependent on how we interpret things. Basically, if we think we're unhappy, we are unhappy, and if we think we're happy, we're happy.

If you experience certain dissatisfactions and interpret them to mean that you must be unhappy, then you are unhappy. An alternative approach would be to assume that your feelings of dissatisfaction might be a helpful and positive signal that you are meant to *improve* your life. With this perspective, you can be happy, even amidst your dissatisfactions. With a positive frame of mind, you can also work more effectively to alleviate the sources of your dissatisfactions, whether those sources are outer circumstances or your own inner habits.

In fact, many seekers begin their spiritual search because they have experienced some dissatisfaction with their lives, and want to feel more satisfied, complete, positive, whole, and happy. Therefore, rather than interpreting a sense of dissatisfaction as a sign of unavoidable unhappiness, you can choose to view it in a positive light – perhaps as a sign that you are growing and being prodded to create an outer world that better reflects and nourishes your evolving soul.

Why is Happiness So Elusive?

Oh, you hate your job? Why didn't you say so? There's a support group for that. It's called EVERYBODY, and they meet at the bar.
—**Drew Carey**

There is so much suffering in this world; many people don't seem to be as happy as they'd like to be. Those who don't have enough are struggling just to survive, while those who have all the comforts of life may find themselves becoming self-absorbed, spoiled, or worried about losing what they have. Many people are living frantic lives, with little time available for simpler pleasures, such as appreciating the beauty of nature, sharing blessed moments with loved ones, or quietly enjoying the peaceful throb of being alive.

Instead, large multitudes are rushing through cities and towns around the globe, getting themselves in all kinds of messes. Some are trying to dig their way out of financial debt, while others are making arrangements for a marriage or a divorce – or perhaps a second or third marriage or divorce. Parents are speeding home from work so they can get the kids to ballet class on time, in between the football tryouts and the cheerleading practice — driving here and there, and perhaps picking up some bags of fast food on the way home. Many find themselves barely making it through each day in time to get a few hours of sleep before getting up to do it all again. With so much to do, who has time to find happiness?

Even those who seem to have all that a good life can offer can find themselves far from the happiness they seek. Abd Er-Rahman III, Sultan of Spain in the tenth century, spoke of the elusiveness of happiness while describing what one would think to have been among the happiest of lives:

> *"I have now reigned about 50 years in victory or peace, beloved by my subjects, dreaded by my enemies, and respected by my allies. Riches and honors, power and pleasure, have waited on my call, nor does any earthly blessing appear to have been wanting to my felicity. In this situation, I have diligently numbered the days of pure and genuine happiness which have fallen to my lot. They amount to fourteen."*

Several years ago, I learned an intriguing lesson about the nature of happiness while editing a video commercial about a discount store in one of the poorest areas in Southern California. Most of the customers interviewed for this video were Mexican immigrants who barely got by on minimal wages. These were not the kind of elegant or well-dressed folks that you'd usually see on a commercial. Some of them were way overdue for a haircut, while others could have used some heavy-duty dental work. The video production crew had approached these customers on their way in or out of the store, and asked them to share their thoughts about having a place where they could purchase second-rate clothes and home goods for a fraction of what they'd have to pay in larger stores.

What struck me most was to see how many of these folks were simply, genuinely, and sincerely happy. You could see it in their faces. You could feel the sincerity of their happiness, as these humble immigrants beamed big, beautiful smiles, in spite of a few missing teeth here and there. You could imagine many of them going home after a hard day's work, spending time with their families and friends, and celebrating their simple lives while knowing they are loved. Obviously, each one had their own individual stories, but from their faces, I could catch a glimpse into their challenging but happy lives.

It was striking for me to see such bright faces in contrast to all the producers and technicians working with me on the video. Here we were, being paid quite well with fairly cushy jobs, and none of us had nearly as bright and happy faces as these so-called "poor" folks!

> *Money can buy the husk of things, but not the kernel.*
> *It brings you food but not appetite, medicine but not*
> *health, acquaintances but not friends, servants but not*
> *faithfulness, days of joy but not peace or happiness.*
> —**Henrik Ibsen**

Ultimately, happiness is elusive due to misguided ideas about what happiness truly is, and how it can be nurtured. After all, how many of us have really contemplated what happiness is? We put so much time and effort – first into years of schoolwork, and then into toiling long hours for our households and workplaces. Yet, how much time have we actually put into contemplating what thoughts and actions will create greater happiness in our lives and in the world? When is the last time you really sat quietly and contemplated what happiness means to you?

In fact, when I was first asked to write this book, an old, forgotten, curmudgeonly, monastic mindset inside of me became somewhat annoyed, thinking, "Happiness? Happiness? What do I have to do with happiness?!? I'm an ascetic! I'm too busy being spiritual to bother with being happy!"

Along with this bit of monastic curmudgeonry, I was also very happy to be asked to write about such a beneficial and fruitful topic. I'd had the blessing of spending time with a number of very happy spiritual beings – including my two spiritual guides, or gurus, who had shown me that spiritual attainment can indeed come along with great happiness.

As my contemplations and preparations for this book continued, I also began to recognize more clearly that happiness is, and has always been, right inside my heart and soul, as it most certainly also exists fully inside of you. This is the level of happiness that I want to unfold with you in this book.

Happiness Comes From Within

Men and women are rushing hither and thither in the blind search for happiness, and cannot find it; nor ever will until they recognize that happiness is already within them and round about them, filling the universe, and that they, in their selfish searching, are shutting themselves out from it.
—James Allen

The first step in finding happiness is to understand that happiness always comes from inside yourself. Even if your experience of happiness appears to be coming from an outer source or experience, the actual happiness is coming from within you.

Happiness arises from within us, and dances with whatever appears to be bringing those apparently outer enjoyments. This inner-outer happiness dance may create the illusion that your happiness is actually coming from the outer enjoyments, however it is not.

This becomes clear when we discover that certain situations that had once brought great happiness no longer create the same effect. Time and time again, each of us is given opportunities to learn and remember that it is not outer things that bring happiness, but the interactions of our inner thoughts and feelings with those things. Our inner thoughts and feelings are the basis of both our happiness and our unhappiness.

Because happiness comes from within, even when things don't appear to be going perfectly well outwardly, it is still possible to experience sincere happiness. It is our inner feeling that creates happiness, along with how we interpret the events of life. For one person, breaking a leg may be a horrible and unhappy tragedy, while for another it may be a trophy of great honor.

Several years ago, I was shopping at an office supply store, when my car's license plate number was read over the loudspeaker. It turned out that a woman had just dented my fairly new car in the parking lot. The woman either didn't have insurance or didn't want to use it for some reason, so she offered to personally pay for the repair costs, and gave me a phone number for where she worked – at a nearby Denny's restaurant.

As soon as I drove away, I could feel that I didn't really want to take this woman's hard-earned money just to fix a bit of cosmetic damage. I mean, the car still ran fine, and I couldn't even see the dent while driving. Why, the dent would even make my car easier to spot in parking lots, and would probably lower its theft value as well. But mostly, I just didn't want to take money unnecessarily from someone who obviously worked very hard for every dollar. I wanted to forgive my debtor just as I wished God to always forgive me.

When I phoned to tell the woman this decision, she argued at first, but eventually conceded to *not* paying for the damage. How wonderful it is to create a situation where two people in a car incident can be arguing about wanting the other person to be okay. This is a great example of how one generous spirit can bring that same higher level of response from others, and perhaps eventually uplift the whole world.

The woman and I both walked away from this experience feeling blessed. And now, whenever I see the dent – which is still there after nearly ten years – I feel a sense of happiness rather than upset. I get to remember my own kindness rather than feeling a sense of loss. If the dent had been there because I bumped into someone else's car, or from an accident with a lot of anger and conflict, then I most certainly would have wanted it to be fixed up right away so as not to be reminded of an unhappy memory every time I saw my car.

This story shows how happiness is ultimately all in the interpretation. Any outer situation can be either a source of happiness or unhappiness, because happiness comes from within ourselves.

Are You Already Happy?

Most people are about as happy as they make up their minds to be.
— Abraham Lincoln

Did you ever think that you might be happy and not know it? Maybe this is IT! Maybe you just need a diploma of happiness like the college diploma the Wizard of Oz gave to the scarecrow, or a happiness medal like the medal of honor that made the lion recognize his own true courage. Congratulations, you are now officially a happy person!

Being happy doesn't mean that you have to act like some carbon-copy cyborg of smileyness. You can be happy while enjoying whatever role you are playing – flowing and growing while being whoever you are, however you are, and wherever you are. Some people may even find happiness in being somewhat of a curmudgeon. In fact, quite a few journalists and media personalities have made fortunes from doing just that!

Just imagine – what would it feel like to simply accept and believe that you are already, always, automatically, deeply and profoundly happy, and to know that you will always inherently be happy, regardless of what does or doesn't happen in your life?

Sometimes happiness can boil down to whether we think we are happy, therefore, please don't confuse your happiness with things that may or may not be out of sorts in your life. Remember that every life will inevitably have ups and downs. With this awareness, let the waves of your life come and go, and seek to maintain a happy spirit through it all.

Don't be swept away by how others might interpret a challenging situation. Take the reins of your mind, and choose to affirm your natural state of happiness. Learn to enjoy all the twists and turns that come with being alive as you, on this planet, and at this time.

Start with the assumption that you are already happy, and you'll have taken an amazing and powerful step to being happy. By accepting that you're already happy, you'll be relieving yourself of a great burden – that of always seeking and desiring to find happiness in external people, places and things. You'll sigh with relief, while relaxing deeply into the arms of your own natural state of happiness.

After all, being too needy for happiness can have the same effect on your happiness that being needy about money can have on your finances – it can weaken your sense of self-empowerment. If you spend all your energy fervently seeking happiness, it may elude you. The very act of desperately seeking happiness may keep you from being happy; and the more you constantly ask yourself if you are happy, the less happy you may become.

This is one reason why those who think they're not feeling happy are often advised to focus their attention on observing someone who *is* happy, or on helping someone else to find greater happiness. While admiring or helping others, our focus is on appreciating and serving, instead of on monitoring our own personal, momentary experiences of happiness. Remember, a watched "happiness pot" never boils!

Put your efforts into helping others, and, voila! You just may slip into the ocean of happiness that exists beneath the part of your mind that had been so desperately seeking to grasp a mere mirage of momentary happiness.

On this journey of spiritual happiness, let's start by assuming that we are already, essentially, happy. Then our task is not so much to create something that isn't there, but to uncover and discover what already is.

Different Folks, Different Strokes

Before jumping into the refreshing waters of spiritual happiness, let's visit what some great thinkers and philosophers have said about what happiness is, what brings greater happiness, whether happiness is worth seeking, and where happiness exists.

What is happiness?

> *The full use of your powers along lines of excellence.*
> —definition of "happiness" by John F. Kennedy

Happiness is the way of travel—not a destination.
—Roy M. Goodman

Happiness is having a large, loving, caring, close-knit family in another city.
—George Burns

Happiness is a butterfly, which, when pursued, is always just beyond your grasp, but which, if you will set down quietly, may alight upon you.
—Nathaniel Hawthorne

True happiness is.... to enjoy the present, without anxious dependence upon the future.
—Seneca

What brings greater happiness?

The ingredients of happiness are so simple that they can be counted on one hand. First of all, happiness must be shared. Selfishness is its enemy; to make another happy is to be happy one's self. It is quiet, seldom found for long in crowds, most easily won in moments of solitude and reflection. It comes from within, and rests most securely on simple goodness and clear conscience.
—William Ogden

Happiness... it lies in the joy of achievement, in the thrill of creative effort.
—Vincent Van Gogh

Whoever possesses God is happy.
—Augustine

Men's happiness and misery depends altogether as much upon their own humor as it does upon fortune.
—François, Duc De La Rochefoucauld

Doing good is the greatest happiness.
—Chinese proverb

To find out what one is fitted to do and to secure an opportunity to do it is the key to happiness.
—John Dewey

Happy are those who find wisdom... She is more precious than jewels, and nothing you desire can compare with her. Her ways are ways of pleasantness, and all her paths are peace.
—Torah

People who recommend happiness

I believe that the very purpose of life is to be happy.
—Dalai Lama

Be happy while you're living, for you're a long time dead.
—Scottish Proverb

The superior man is always happy.
—Confucius

Nobody really cares if you're miserable, so you might as well be happy.
—Cynthia Nelms

The good of mankind means the attainment, by every man, of all the happiness which he can enjoy without diminishing the happiness of his fellow men.
—Thomas Henry Huxley

Happiness is the only sanction of life; where happiness fails, existence remains a mad and lamentable experiment.
—George Santayana

People who don't like happiness

> *The "pursuit of happiness" is responsible for a good part of the ills and miseries of the modern world.*
> —Malcolm Muggeridge

> *Only the spirit of rebellion craves for happiness in this life. What right have we human beings to happiness?*
> —Henrik Ibsen

> *Happiness serves hardly any other purpose than to make unhappiness possible.*
> —Marcel Proust

> *Extreme happiness begets tragedy.*
> —Chinese proverb

> *Happiness is a monstrosity! Punished are those who seek it.*
> —Gustave Flaubert

Happiness is easy

> *If a man is unhappy, remember that his unhappiness is his own fault, for God made all men to be happy.*
> —Epictetus

> *If there were in the world today any large number of people who desired their own happiness more than they desired the unhappiness of others, we could have paradise in a few years.*
> —Bertrand Russell

> *Being unconditionally happy is a practice: "Come what may, today I'm going to smile. Anyway, everything is going to die! Everything is going to vanish and disappear—so what! Who cares! Let me at least be happy, smile this moment, enjoy my very breath."*
> —Sri Sri Ravi Shankar

Most happiness is overlooked because it doesn't cost anything.
—**William Ogden**

Happiness is impossible to capture

The pursuit of happiness is a most ridiculous phrase; if you pursue happiness you'll never find it.
—**C. P. Snow**

Perfect happiness is the absence of the striving for happiness.
—**Chuang Tsu**

A great obstacle to happiness is to expect too much happiness.
—**Bernard Fontanelle**

The search for happiness ... always ends in the ghastly sense of the bottomless nothingness into which you will inevitably fall if you strain any further.
—**D.H. Lawrence**

Happiness lies outside

It is in the love of one's family only that heartfelt happiness is known.
—**Thomas Jefferson**

A comfortable house is a great source of happiness. It ranks immediately after health and a good conscience.
—**Sydney Smith**

It's not money that brings happiness, it's lots of money.
—**Russian saying**

All happiness depends on a leisurely breakfast.
—**John Gunther**

My whole working philosophy is that the only stable happiness for mankind is that it shall live married in blessed union to woman-kind—intimacy, physical and psychical between a man and his wife. I wish to add that my state of bliss is by no means perfect.
—D.H. Lawrence

Happiness dwells within

Happiness is your nature. It is not wrong to desire it. What is wrong is seeking it outside when it is inside.
—Ramana Maharshi

You must try to generate happiness within yourself. If you aren't happy in one place, chances are you won't be happy anyplace.
—Ernie Banks

The foolish man seeks happiness in the distance; the wise man grows it under his feet.
—James Oppenheim

I am happy even before I have a reason.
—Hafiz

This world is mortal. You have to attain the immortal happiness. If you don't attain the eternal joy in this mortal world, then your life is in vain.
—Baba Muktananda

Section Two:
Introducing Spiritual Happiness

Coining the Term *Spiritual Happiness*

Every now and then, words have to be redefined and clarified, having become muddied and obscured by too many uses as patches for words that don't exist in our culture. The word happiness is like the word love — what does love really mean? What does success mean? Can you tell if someone has love by the number of people in their life? Can you tell if someone is successful by how much money they have?

Just as Hawaiians have many words for rain, but most mainlanders are willing to call just about anything from the gentlest sun shower to massively powerful thunderstorms "rain," in the same way, I'd like to introduce and unfold a new, more specific happiness term for you — *spiritual happiness.*

With spiritual happiness, you are not waiting to be rich before you can be happy, or to find the right person to be happy, or to have more friends to be happy. You don't need to look differently to be spiritually happy; nor do you have to heal all your flaws to be spiritually happy.

With spiritual happiness, you can look at the world with realistic eyes — seeing, experiencing, and responding to all the muddled mess that life can sometimes seem to be. Yet, in the depths of your being, you'll know a peacefulness and contentment that never fades, even while the world may be crashing down around you.

With spiritual happiness:

- You are working in harmony with the universe and your own highest good

- You can surf the ups and downs of life with the blessing of knowing that you're growing.

- You enjoy a good sense of humor that makes even bitter medicines go down more easily.

Spiritual happiness is unconditional happiness. Spiritual happiness comes with a sense of eternal hope and a trust in universal perfection. With spiritual happiness, you can be ecstatic even when you're miserable, because you know that whatever troubles have come your way are meant to uplift your soul in the long run. With spiritual happiness, you can feel complete even when you lose something valuable; you can be fearless even while shaking in your boots.

If I were to boil the whole idea of spiritual happiness down to one word, I would have to say that the essence of spiritual happiness is *faith*. Not blind faith, or ignorant faith, or a one-time declaration of some faithful-sounding phrase, but true faith – a powerful yet tender trust that is drenched in qualities such as wisdom, humility, love, courage and service. This faith comes with a greater awareness of spiritual principles, and seeks to be in harmony with the Tao, the flow, the Shakti, the perfect divine pattern, and the Will of God – all words used to describe the supreme energy and consciousness that is beyond word and thought.

Faith is not only a refuge during troubling times, but can also help empower us to create an outer life that is in greater harmony with our nature. This faith can come with vast knowledge or with simple wisdom – or perhaps with both together. True faith knows that everything is always fine, right here, right now, and forever. Everything is fine when it feels fine, and everything is also fine when it doesn't feel so fine. Faith knows that life is a gift, always.

Faith is a combination of: "May the force be with you" and "May *you* be with the force!" Faith keeps away bad guys like self-sabotage, fear, anger, and depression. Faith is the grand elixir of spiritual happiness.

The Difference Between Relative and Spiritual Happiness

First, I'll describe three basic levels of regular old relative happiness:

1. **Body-based:** This lowest level of relative happiness relates to the more animalistic nature of human beings, such as experiences of happiness that come from the satisfaction of raw desires. People who are stuck in this level of happiness tend to be ravenous and are always looking for immediate pleasures, without much regard for troubling consequences.

2. **Mind-based:** The second level of relative happiness involves a bit more intelligence. You look to create a good life, and are willing to forgo some of the more animalistic, instinctual, and self-indulgent pleasures in order to achieve greater long-term happiness. For example, you're willing to go to work every day so you can have a home and enjoy the good things in life.

3. **Heart-based:** The third level of happiness has more of a spiritual element. You've purified your understanding, awareness, and motives enough that your happiness comes from

30

greater things, such as love, devotion, and service to humanity and to those you love. In this level, you may also begin to taste the nectar of spiritual happiness streaming forth.

Beyond these three levels of relative happiness exists the realm of spiritual happiness.

Spiritual happiness is a deep contentment and joy that exists peacefully beneath all the superficial waves of ephemeral life. Spiritual happiness comes from having a greater vision of how you fit into the bigger universal picture. Spiritual happiness brings a sense of gratitude and faith that allows you to dance beneath, above, and throughout the ups and downs of life.

One way to describe spiritual happiness would be to say that ordinary happiness comes from getting what you want, while spiritual happiness comes from wanting what you get. Ordinary happiness depends mostly on what happens in arenas that may be beyond your control, while spiritual happiness is potentially in your court.

Spiritual happiness shines most brightly when we are in harmony with God and the universal flow. Instead of waiting for God and the universal flow to get in harmony with *us*, we can take a more proactive stance and create the intention to become in greater harmony with God's will and the flow of nature.

You can use whatever religious or non-religious image or term you choose for envisioning this unknowable perfect flow of God's will. What is most important for supporting and nurturing your experience of spiritual happiness is the state of mind that comes from seeking to be in universal harmony.

Spiritual happiness is ultimately up to how you look at things. Another tangible way to shift into spiritual happiness is to train ourselves to be grateful for everything that has or has not come into our lives. Of course, this exercise is easy to do for the good things that are in keeping with our desires, however, even tough times can be deserving of our gratitude when we are living from a higher, more spiritually awakened awareness.

Spiritual happiness involves entering a bigger picture view, in which we can see the ups and downs of life as paint strokes on this magnificent canvas that is our own individual and unique story.

With spiritual happiness, we trust in universal goodness, while resting in the humility of knowing that we see only tiny slivers of a grand and infinite reality. With humility and trust, we can stop living life as a tug of war with Universal Reality. While striving to flow in harmony with the unknowable essence of life, we walk lightly, yet powerfully upon this earth. We can more easily let go of whatever falls away, and embrace whatever comes with a happy heart.

Who so trusteth in the LORD, happy is he.
– Proverbs

Having spiritual happiness doesn't necessarily mean that you walk around letting anything fall upon you without making any efforts to also create what you want. It's a balance. You put forth sincere efforts, and if some of your efforts don't bear fruit, you nevertheless have faith that all is well, that everything ultimately happens for the best, and that God will provide whatever you need at the right time, and in the right way.

From a stance of faith and surrender, we are able to act with confidence, patience, and a positive attitude. Because positive interpretations of the events we experience can actually help to create positive outcomes, finding our natural state of spiritual happiness and optimism is bound to bring unexpected blessings into many areas of our lives.

Spiritual happiness will also offer great peace when it is time to leave this world. In fact, one of the most precious qualities of spiritual happiness is that it will stay with you at the moment of your death (but don't wait until then to look for it!). With spiritual happiness, you'll be able to depart from this life journey with a deep sense of gratitude and satisfaction, rather than weeping and lamenting with guilt and disappointment over the past, or with fear of the unknown abyss ahead. You'll be waving farewell, while moving forward courageously and happily into the great light of your Beloved, of Heaven, and of your own sublime soul.

The treasure of spiritual happiness is available to us with just a few shifts of understanding, a bit of expansion in our awareness, and some refinement of our thoughts and actions. This is what many great spiritual philosophers have declared, and it has also been an ongoing lesson and experience on my path.

Spiritual Happiness and the Happiness Hierarchy

Here's a chart that was inspired by psychologist Abraham Maslow's *hierarchy of needs* chart. This is one view of where spiritual happiness might fit in with other kinds of happiness:

```
              /\
         Eternal Bliss
          /  6  \
      Spiritual Happiness
          /  5  \
       Creative Happiness
         /   4   \
       Mental Happiness
         /   3    \
      Emotional Happiness
        /    2      \
       Physical Happiness
      /       1        \
```

It's not so much that we need to "finish" each level before moving on to the next higher levels of happiness. We can have *spiritual happiness* even without having some of the levels beneath it – such as physical happiness, emotional happiness and mental happiness. In fact, many monastics and sages throughout the ages have chosen to live a life of physical, emotional, or mental austerity specifically to find their way to greater heights of spiritual happiness – although others have managed to find a way to have it all. I'll describe each level as I'm picturing it in this chart:

1. **Physical Happiness:** Physical happiness means having the basics that will allow you to survive and thrive, such as food, water, shelter, and air.

2. **Emotional Happiness:** Emotional happiness comes from feelings of love, belonging, and having a sense of family or community.

3. **Mental Happiness:** Mental happiness comes with a positive self-image, and includes making good use of your mind's ability to continually improve and grow in your understanding and appreciation of life.

4. **Creative Happiness:** Creative happiness blossoms forth when you are expressing your excellence as whatever you are meant to be – being the best artist, manager, cook, friend, mother, or worker that you can be – offering your creative efforts to benefit society and those you love.

5. **Spiritual Happiness:** Spiritual happiness fills you with the peacefulness of unshakable faith, as you rest in your higher self — while giving and serving with universal love and a vision of the bigger picture of your soul's journey.

6. **Eternal Bliss:** Eternal bliss is a realm of unearthly ecstasy and oneness with all. We'll know it when we see it!

What Spiritual Happiness Isn't

Spiritual happiness is not just a particular way of looking or acting. You can't always tell right away who is or isn't spiritually happy just by their outer appearance. For example, spiritual happiness doesn't mean that you have to walk around smiling all the time and jumping up and down with glee, although there is nothing wrong with smiling or jumping up and down with glee.

Although spiritual happiness does tend to shine through visibly in your face and your life, being spiritually happy doesn't necessarily mean that *everyone* has to *always* know that you are spiritually happy. For example, if you are a spiritually happy elementary school teacher with an unruly class, you may have to demonstrate what appears to be anger or sternness at times in order to control and guide your students. Yet, even then, you can still be completely spiritually happy and comfortably identified with the deep soul witness that always enjoys the show.

Another reason that you may sometimes choose to be happy and know it, but not "clap your hands and show it," can be due to responses you may have received while expressing happiness in the past. Some people may have interpreted your happiness as a sign of foolishness. Others may have responded to your happiness with jealousy, or may have even interpreted your happiness as a personal insult to them (people are funny creatures). In fact, there are some people who – seeing someone who is happy – will test the person, and try to bring him or her back down into "not-so-happy land with the rest of us."

Therefore, remember that you don't always have to *look* massively happy to *be* massively happy!

The Theories Behind Spiritual Happiness

The main theory behind spiritual happiness is that everything is divine, everything is a gift from God, and everything is your own deepest consciousness bursting forth into a phenomenal life experience that is ultimately your creation, and in a sense, your life-dream.

Remember the nursery rhyme, "Row, row, row your boat, gently down the stream; merrily, merrily, merrily, merrily, life is but a dream?" As this song teaches, once you know that life is but a dream, you will be able to row your boat — not just merrily, but *merrily, merrily, merrily, merrily* down the stream. That's spiritual happiness!

Spiritual happiness comes from having a bigger, more long-term view of life, within which our inevitable ups and downs can be seen as hills and valleys amidst a vast, ever changing landscape. With the vision of spiritual happiness, we trust in universal grace and perfection – even while acknowledging that there is much we don't know about how "IT" all works.

In today's desire- and commercial-based society, spiritual happiness is somewhat of an acquired taste. External-based happiness can often seem to be more tangible than the deep, inner stream of spiritual happiness. After all, outer triggers of happiness are easier to find. They're what most of us are used to. Something good happens today, and we feel happy today. If something good doesn't happen tomorrow, then we'll be hungry for another shot of outer happiness. Outer happiness is like a drug or junk food — it's quick and easy, but not always good for our ultimate well-being.

Spiritual happiness, on the other hand, is a delicacy that can only be tasted by a tongue that has lowered its dependence on the "cayenne pepper" of worldly pleasures. Therefore, we may have to lower our emotional dependence on worldly pleasures before our "happiness sensors" can become refined enough to taste the more delicate flavors of spiritual happiness.

One of the main secrets of spiritual happiness is to make positive use of the immense power of your mind, your thoughts, and the way you view the world. If you trust that everything that comes to you is somehow a blessing, that very trust will to help to make it so. Your trust in the blessing is a blessing in and of itself.

A positive and optimistic view of life is essential for true spiritual happiness, with faith and trust in the loving hand of universal grace that is always there to hold us and guide our steps.

Upgrading Your Spiritual Happiness Software

The transition into spiritual happiness is kind of like upgrading yourself, as you might upgrade some software on your computer. You put a new disk in, and the installation program goes through your drives and folders to clean them out and prepare your system for a whole new program and experience – in this case, the experience of spiritual happiness. After taking out whatever is no longer needed, the installation program then puts in the appropriate replacements and upgrades.

If you are locking your folders of anger, resentment, fear, and unhappiness by refusing to grow out of your current status, well then, the installation disk won't be able to properly upgrade your computer program, or your spiritual happiness program. Therefore, in your computer as well as in life, you have to let go of the old to bring in the new.

Once the installation has taken place, the next time you start up that program, it's a whole new look — with new icons and new capabilities to explore. It's exciting. You may have some little soft spot of missing the look of the old version, because you had gotten used to it, but you eventually learn to let go of those attachments and to embrace the new version. Eventually, the new version becomes even more comfortable and familiar than the earlier one was.

This is a metaphor for what it is like to upgrade your vision into one of spiritual happiness. Everything becomes affected — your thoughts, actions, interpretations, and life circumstances. It's upgrading to a better, happier *you*.

You may find that this upgrade to spiritual happiness inspires you to interpret and respond differently to various experiences in your life. Please allow these transformations to happen. One of the biggest obstacles to spiritual growth and happiness must be our tendency to hold on to old habits and identifications.

Learn to let go of who you thought you were, and who others think you are, and seek to find your purest self — the *you* that you've always wished would be you.

Spiritual Happiness in Action

If you have a long face and a chip on your shoulder, if you are not radiant with joy and friendliness, if you are not filled to overflowing with love and goodwill for all beings.... one thing is certain: you do not know God.
—**Peace Pilgrim**

Peace Pilgrim is one of the best examples of spiritual happiness in action that I've encountered. I never actually met her in person, but recently spent a year scripting and editing a one-hour documentary about Peace Pilgrim's life, and do feel as though I know her fairly well.

Peace wasn't always the perfect example of spiritual happiness. Her childhood was quite pleasant, as were her teenage years. But then she married a fellow who turned out to be living on a very different level of awareness and spiritual maturity than the one she was quickly evolving into.

Mildred – which was her name before becoming "Peace Pilgrim" – had been through a great deal of spiritual maturation in her youth. At a very young age, she took the golden rule, "do unto others as you would have them do unto you," as a personal motto. While watching war mentalities taking hold of the world and seeing aggressions such as McCarthyism running rampant in the United States, Mildred became more and more dedicated to the cause of bringing peace to the world.

Mildred's husband, Stanley, had really only wanted a domestic wife who could cook and make babies, and soon discovered that he hadn't exactly gotten his right "wife order" in. Mildred was proud, strong-willed, opinionated, stubborn, and certainly not docile – nor was she interested in cooking or making babies. She wanted to help create world peace.

When the United States Army drafted Stanley, Mildred asked him not to go. She said that if he went to the camp, she would not visit him or have anything to do with him while he was there. Stanley chose to serve, in spite of her request. One of his officers read a letter that Mildred had sent, and told Stanley that her words were grounds for divorce. Soon, Mildred was single again, and became even more actively dedicated to the cause of peace.

At one point, Mildred had gone for a walk deep into the woods, in a disturbed state of mind. She prayed to God, walked, prayed some more, and continued walking. She cried out, "Take me! Take all that I am. I withhold nothing!" And she meant it. The ears of the universe always hear when we really mean it.

During this walking prayer, Mildred had a vision of walking across the country as a penniless pilgrim in the name of peace. She even saw the map of her future routes through each state in her mind's eye. After this vision came many more years of life lessons and personal growth, until the time finally came for Mildred to bring her vision to life. At age forty-four, she shed her outer life and became completely identified with and dedicated to her inspired cause.

She would be a peace pilgrim, traveling the country, and touching person after person with her kindness, wisdom, and passion for peace. One by one, she would change the world. She put on a blue tunic with the words "Peace Pilgrim" sewn into the front and "Walking Coast to Coast for World Disarmament" on the back, and walked out of the door of her house, leaving Mildred behind. From now on, she was living in faith. She was Peace Pilgrim (hear her roar!) The year was 1953.

Peace spent nearly thirty years walking back and forth across the country seven times – taking roundabout routes that brought her into every major city, and through Mexico and Canada as well. Her vow was to remain a pilgrim until mankind had learned the way of peace, eating only when food was offered, and sleeping only where shelter was offered – although sometimes she would sleep in a field or by a bus stop. She would not ask for either food or shelter; they had to be offered. How's that for dramatically upping your level of faith? And it worked.

People would see Peace Pilgrim walking by, and would ask about the words on her tunic. She would eagerly tell them about how the world is so in need of peace, and how we can each help by creating peace within ourselves and in our own lives.

Peace Pilgrim had found what she called her comfortable "need level," (which obviously differs for everyone). In fulfillment of her faith, all of Peace's needs were provided for nearly three decades, until her death in 1981 in a car accident on a rural road, during a rare car ride to one of her early morning speaking engagements.

From the day Peace began her pilgrimage, all she owned was one set of clothes, a pair of shoes, a toothbrush, a comb, and a pen. As she told one high school class, with her arms raised in freedom, "This is me, with all my earthly possessions. If I want to travel somewhere, I just stand up and begin walking!" Can you imagine being so happy without a house, without health insurance, without a car, without money for your next meal, and without a second pair of shoes? Yet, Peace used to often exclaim, "I have health, happiness, and peace — things you couldn't buy if you were a billionaire!"

Peace was living in harmony with her deepest longings and fulfilling her greatest potential. In India's philosophical terms, Peace Pilgrim was living in accordance with her personal and individual *dharma* of being a wandering sage for peace. Living in harmony with our true and most righteous nature is called *dharma* in the Sanskrit language, and dharma is a great path to walk in the land of spiritual happiness.

Wherever Peace Pilgrim went, she would fascinate the media. While scripting and editing the documentary about her life, I sorted through hundreds of enthusiastic newspaper articles and newsreel stories about her.

Peace didn't start a huge organization with thousands of employees to propagate her message, yet her message found its way into the world gently and steadily — through radio interviews, television interviews, and while giving inspirational lectures and discussions in every possible kind of church and school. Although many wanted to follow along on her pilgrimage, Peace maintained her freedom. She would give her love and wisdom in one place, and walk on freely to love and give some more in the next.

During Peace's 28-year pilgrimage, the world did become more peaceful, due to her efforts, along with the efforts of other peacemakers. The earlier glory of war and fighting began to fade into an increasing universal wish for world peace. Although the world still struggles with issues of war and peace to this day, Peace Pilgrim truly demonstrated just how powerful a majority of one can be in helping to uplift the consciousness of a person, a city, a country, and the whole world. As she would often say, "If you want to make peace, you must be peaceful."

Peace Pilgrim's mission was fueled by spiritual happiness, along with dedication, service, optimism, and extraordinary faith. You could hardly ever find Peace without a beautiful smile on her face and a joyful cadence to her walk.

Eventually, Peace's hair turned totally white, and her face was covered with the creases of age – especially after walking outside in the sun for three decades. Nevertheless, when you see her on the television screen, she has the freshness and exuberance of a child. She moves with freedom, and sings out her message without fear of revealing her deep wisdom and innocent faith. Peace Pilgrim is a great example of someone who found the ever-flowing stream of spiritual happiness and dove right in, in her own unique and individual way.

Of course, very few people are called to live such an austere or eccentric life. Your job is to find your own simple or dramatic path to personal fulfillment and spiritual happiness.

Section Three:
The Secrets

In this section, you'll find many secrets that can help bring greater spiritual happiness into your life. Please accept and enjoy them as offerings in the spirit of friendship and service. Don't worry if you disagree with some of my offerings. I don't assume to have the final, definitive stand on all the secrets of spiritual happiness. Rather, I've chosen to include some specific secrets that have been part of my own life lessons — the fruits from my personal research and experiences, blessed and guided by the hand of Grace that thrives on our aspirations to be of service.

I hope and pray that these words and stories will be useful tools for you in unfolding your own personal path to spiritual happiness.

Relax!

When someone is impatient and says, "I haven't got all day," I always wonder, how can that be? How can you not have all day?
– George Carlin

The first secret of spiritual happiness is to stop running everywhere all the time! Change your schedule, change your life, and see how much you're able to simplify things. Stop and consider whether all the activities that fill your days are truly necessary, beneficial, or even enjoyable. If you spend all your days doing unnecessary things that waste your precious time and energy, then you won't have enough time and energy to devote to what would make you more spiritually happy.

If your schedule is too full to allow any spaces of peaceful enjoyment and reflection, then consider thinning out your schedule. Maybe your kids would also rather spend some quiet time with you, and not just get home and turn on the TV because everyone's too exhausted to do anything else. See if you can create more space in your life by thinning out your schedule if it is too busy, or by considering other ways to simplify your life.

In fact, if your life is simpler, then your expenses will probably also be less. You won't need to be running around doing as much extra work just to get enough money to pay for all the costs that are required to maintain a busy, frantic life.

Some people's lives are so action-packed that the only time they really get to take a break is when they must stop and sit in the bathroom. In fact, some people I know have actually turned their bathroom into a kind of rest and reading room. One friend even memorized an entire set of Trivial Pursuits Q&A cards in the bathroom, so he could win when we played.

Truthfully, you can create inner space any place where you can take a few moments to sit quietly and enjoy some peaceful contemplation, devotion, and rest. Find places for spaces in your day. Get in the habit of taking pauses to calm the waves of worldly concern, and strive to sanctify every moment and each action with a peaceful approach.

Breathe deeply, and with ease.

A crust eaten in peace is better than a banquet partaken
in anxiety.
– **Aesop**

There are many ways to create more inner space. Here is a contemplation practice that you can do right now, or anytime:

Sit quietly, and allow all your thoughts to soften. Watch the flow of your breath as it moves in, and as it moves out, as it moves in, and as it moves out.

Allow your body to relax fully. Calm the waves of your mind, quiet the adrenaline rush of your day, and focus your attention inside – toward the center of spiritual happiness in your divine, pure, unsullied soul. See your soul shining brightly like a golden star in the center of your being.

Now, repeat the word "happiness" as you breathe in, and "happiness" as you breathe out. Symbolically receive happiness from this universe, and offer your happiness back with love. Think, feel, and breathe happiness.

Remember that even a few minutes of peaceful sitting can make a huge difference in how you feel and in how you approach each day.

Inspire Your Atmosphere

Though we travel the world over to find the beautiful,
we must carry it with us or we find it not.
– **Ralph Waldo Emerson**

I first learned about the practice of creating an inspiring atmosphere during my twenties, while living in an Indian *ashram,* or monastery.

Every here and there were heartwarming sights, sounds, and smells to remind us to think of God and the spiritual nature of life. Rooms and hallways were filled with uplifting photos and statues, and we had many temples and other holy sacred spaces, including powerful "meditation caves" that we could visit for even a few moments in the midst of a busy day.

This sacred environment offered constant reminders for us to take time to realign ourselves with our divine Self and our greatest potential. Pools of restful and invigorating waters were sprinkled throughout each day – moments of peaceful space, through which we could touch the great space of our eternal nature.

Every day, we had morning chanting sessions, noontime prayers, afternoon mantras, and evening services. We'd also be treated to many lectures and discussions about the most sublime and vibrant spiritual teachings you could imagine. These spiritual practices gave time amidst a busy day to turn our attention inward, toward lofty spiritual thoughts and feelings. I might walk into a chanting session feeling tired, but would usually leave it feeling happy and rejuvenated. In fact, chanting has probably been my number one favorite practice for creating inner happiness.

What does it for you? What helps you to feel inspired and rejuvenated? What kinds of images, smells, tastes, and sounds make you happy? Will taking a walk in nature buoy your spirits? How about listening to some good music? Have you tried singing while you wash dishes? Dance around the room! Wherever you are, and whatever you're doing, create an uplifting atmosphere, whenever and however you can.

Some people like to fill an atmosphere with the sight and smell of blooming flowers. Some may bring fragrance into a room with essential oils, by lighting a bit of incense, or by burning some frankincense on a small brick of charcoal in the morning – which is something I like to do because it reminds me of my days in the monastery. Fragrant smells can sanctify an atmosphere, and can be especially conducive to feelings of happiness. You know, the olfactory lobes in our brains are just about the oldest gizmos in there, so smells can affect us on especially primal levels. Therefore, instead of just letting the world bring us whatever smells happen to be floating by, we can also make efforts to design some inspiring smells for our own atmosphere.

I also love to play uplifting music of various genres whenever I'm cleaning, working, resting, or playing at home. And I make sure to have inspiring books around so I can pick them up and read a couple lines here and there during the day, and before going to sleep. Each of us has individual tastes for what inspires us, and for which of our senses – such as sight, hearing, smelling, tasting, and feeling – affect us the most. Notice what inspires you, and bring more of it into your life.

Even if you don't have the freedom to bring an arsenal of inspiration to your workplace, you can certainly include reminders of uplifting and inspiring sounds, sights, and smells right in your own home. You can create greater happiness at home by taking the time and care to put up decorations and photos of what you love and what inspires you – whether breathtaking photographs of nature, inspired paintings, a golden crucifix or other religious symbolism, photos of your loved ones, or whatever uplifting images float your boat, move your heart, and still your soul.

Surround yourself with reminders of what makes you happy. Don't decorate your home just to satisfy the judgments of company you may invite over. Put up what truly moves and inspires you. If your guests think your tastes are a little eccentric, well then, maybe your boldness will inspire them to also expand their own repertoire of expression and appreciation.

I learned to go beyond decorating for other people after I left the monastery and began working as a video editor for one of the most high paced television news shows in Los Angeles. Soon after beginning the job, I was bold enough to place a medium-sized photo of my spiritual teacher, or guru, in my editing bay – right in front of my workspace.

With all the challenges of transitioning from a decade of *monastic* lifestyle to a very *non-monastic* lifestyle, I wanted to see my guru and keep her close to me, even in photo form. In the midst of this exciting and harried news environment, I wanted to be able to look at my guru's face and be soothed, refreshed, and reminded of all that she represents for me, and of all the teachings and blessings I'd received from her. These spiritual strengths were definitely needed for the challenging life experiences at hand.

Looking at that little photo definitely increased my spiritual happiness during the long hours of editing news stories about every possible topic you can imagine, and a few that you probably can't – such as the risqué fare of "sweeps" weeks, when the number of viewers is measured to decide how much money a show can charge for their commercials. You can usually tell when sweeps season is in the air, because there are a lot more sexy and racy stories, and I was assigned to edit some of them. One series was so explicit that people from the newsroom kept coming up to our third-floor editing suite to see if we were really going through such shocking footage. Eventually, the reporter and I put a sign on the door declaring a five-dollar admission charge.

In the previous, monastic decade, I'd produced and edited hundreds of videos about the most sublime spiritual topics, and now the material for my creative works was dramatic footage from the Los Angeles riots of 1991, shocking scenes of bombed out war shelters from George Bush senior's "Line in the Sand" Gulf war, feature packages about "The Prozac Paradox," "Pearl Harbor, 50 Years Later," "Ghosts on the Queen Mary," and "The Academy Awards Specials," along with all the other newsworthy happenings of a city as large, diverse, and exciting as Los Angeles.

Having my guru's photo nearby helped me to find the inner strength to not only rise to the occasion of all these projects, but also to enjoy creating them – and to do my best to present reports and stories with a slant toward seeing the blessings as well as the challenges. Many workers find the same value in keeping photos of their families in their workplace, but in my case, it was a photo of my guru – who represented my connection with God, with divine inspiration, and with my center of spiritual happiness. Therefore, it was worth the occasional ribbing to have her there.

Some of the producers and reporters would joke a bit about my guru photo. Nevertheless, when things hit the fan and we were rushing from my editing bay into another to finish a piece that had to be on the air in 10 minutes, one of the toughest reporters actually insisted that we bring my guru's photo into the other editing bay with us, saying, "We need her for this one!"

In fact, when we fill our environments with what inspires us, we'll also be more likely to help inspire others. We'll be giving, receiving, and nourishing the spiritual happiness in our lives and in the world.

C03

Know Thyself

The indispensable first step to getting the things you want out of life is this: decide what you want.
–**Ben Stein**

One important secret of spiritual happiness is to really know, under-stand, and respect your nature — your own individual blend. We are all great and magnificent demonstrations of God's glory and nature's creative expression. Even though some spiritual folks like to talk about "oneness" and "equality consciousness," these concepts do not mean that everyone has to be the same in every respect. How boring would that be?

Instead, we can honor ourselves by respecting the unique recipe that God used to make each one of us. Rather than fighting our styles and preferences, we can see if there is a way to integrate them into creating a fulfilling life that honors and respects our individual blend. For example, consider what kinds of work are fulfilling for you. What are you good at doing? What do you like to do?

Someone who fixes cars for a living may be envious of someone else who makes a lot more money by running a successful business. Even though fixing cars may be just the key to their happy life, the person may have been swayed by the opinions of this world to think that running a business would be a better career path.

If you like to fix cars and are envious of someone who makes more money by running a business, then you may very well be experiencing envy for a set of circumstances that you would never even want for yourself. I'd guess that many of our envies are for things we wouldn't want even if they came our way. For example, recent decades of tabloid media have shown that even the most enviable celebrities may not be as happy as they appear to be, or as happy as we might imagine they must be.

> *Being a princess isn't all it's cracked up to be.*
> – Princess Diana

Maybe your happiness lies in coming home from work and being completely free from work worries, unlike a person you think you are envious of — who might look like a big shot, but may also be walking around with way too much stress, and working way too many hours to enjoy the simple and peaceful pleasures of life.

Who are you, and why are you here? What is it that you want in life? The more we comprehend our individual natures, and what we may be here to give and receive, the more we can make efforts to bring our outer world in harmony with that vision. Therefore, this secret says, as did the ancient Greek Oracle, "Know Thyself."

An important road to spiritual happiness is to create a life that is in harmony with what our soul is here to give, to receive, and to learn. Our reasons for being here are not firm and clear answers on a multiple choice test, but more like an ongoing essay question that we are writing throughout our lives. Each experience teaches us more about who we are, and each experience also refines who we are.

If you don't know your own nature, then you may be fooled into wanting things that you don't really want, and living a life that is a reaction to what others have, or to what others think you should have. Your mind will first want one thing, then hop to wanting another, and another, until you have a huge pile of tossed arrows of desire – many contradicting one another – using up your time and energy without ever giving the deep satisfaction that comes from dedicated efforts with clear goals and self-knowledge.

Don't wish to be who other people are; wish to be who you truly are. Instead of just automatically wanting what "everyone else" seems to want, contemplate your true nature to find out what you truly want. Notice what interests you most, and what stirs your soul. Happily pursue your dreams with clarity and confidence – always leaving the door open for unexpected twists, turns, and blessings. Follow *your* bliss.

When your personal nature and your outer life are in harmony, then you are successful, no matter what kind of work you do and no matter how much money you earn. Do whatever you do with enthusiasm, dedication, honor, and love. If you can't do this where you are right now, then consider taking a look at whether you are devoting your time and efforts in the right places for you. Figure out what you love to do and find a way to do it. Then, you'll enter a space of spiritual happiness where even time feels timeless and work feels effortless.

If you love what you do, you will never work another
day in your life.
– **Confucius**

❧

Enjoy Being You

Each morning when I awake, I experience again a
supreme pleasure - that of being Salvador Dali.
– **Salvador Dali**

How great you are, and how great your life is. Open the windows, take a brisk walk, breathe deeply, and relish the most basic and beautiful experience of being alive. Even if you have a challenging life, make a decision to appreciate yourself, and to fully enjoy being you, with all that entails.

Don't wait for other people to appreciate you first – it rarely works that way. If your happiness and self-worth are dependent on what others think of you, well then, you're in a precarious position, aren't you? Simply decide that you are wonderful, faults and all. Stand by yourself with love, and from there, you'll also be better able to make positive changes and improvements in your character, actions, and life circumstances.

Consider how you feel when looking at someone you have a crush on, or with whom you're falling in love. Even their faults are cute – at least for a while. You may love the way they play with their hair, or the way they walk, talk, or dance. You may like the way their mouth moves when they're thinking, or how they get quiet when their heart is touched. Or if you have a child, you may delight in how they behave a bit mischievously at times, or how they are curious and like to get into things. You may see the sun reflecting on your child's hair, and think that this must be the perfect angel of God sent down to bless you – at least during the best moments.

Well, you can also love yourself this way. You can appreciate yourself, have a crush on yourself, and view yourself with loving eyes. You can learn to chuckle away your shortcomings, and to find positive interpretations for how your lacks may be helping you to grow, or perhaps for how they may be helping others to grow. You can love being you, just as you are, while still striving to grow into an even greater image of possibility. You can notice the styles you like, and appreciate your individual taste and way of being.

Many times, we may find it easier to focus on someone else's life than our own, so this secret of spiritual happiness is asking us to also pay attention to ourselves, in a positive way.

This doesn't mean that you have to become an egotistical narcissist. People may be afraid of being criticized for paying attention to themselves, because they don't want to be judged as self-absorbed. Certain "political correctness police" seem to think that you should never talk about yourself or think too well or too often about yourself. However, don't let their judgments deter you from focusing on yourself in the right way.

After all, if there is one thing you've got in this world, it's you. You are the divine light of creation, shining through as a very interesting tale – the story of your life. Whether you choose to share your story publicly with others, at least *you* can read and enjoy your own story.

Relish being whoever you are, and you'll find contentment and spiritual happiness in every moment.

ଔ

Remember Who You Really Are

It often happens that I wake up at night and begin to think about a serious problem and decide I must tell the Pope about it. Then I wake up completely and remember that I am the Pope.
– Pope John XXIII

While getting to know who you are and why you are here, you can also remember that your deepest soul essence is beyond your personal appearance, personality, and all the things that people think make up who you are. Even if others don't see into your depths, that doesn't mean *you* should close your eyes to your own greatness.

One technique that can be especially helpful in remembering who you really are is contemplation. Contemplation is more than merely researching a topic. Contemplation is a combination of outer knowledge and inner wisdom. Wisdom is alive inside of you, and with a receptive and trusting stance, you can open the door to experiencing your soul's wisdom on a conscious level. Ask questions of yourself, and ask questions of God. Pay attention to life, and contemplate what it is all about.

Consider why your soul may have been placed — and indeed, may have even *chosen* to be placed — into the circumstances of your life and the qualities of your personality. What kinds of lessons might you be here to learn? Contemplating these questions will lead you into a more powerful space of observing and listening. Instead of fighting life as though it were an adversary, you'll become more patient, surrendered, focused, accepting, loving, wise, and happy.

Remembering who you are is like a person awakening from a dramatic dream to find him- or herself in the coziness of their own bed.

However, in this case, you awaken and enjoy that coziness while still continuing to experience the "dream" of your life.

Imagine that you are both the producer and the audience for the play of your life. You are the creator, observer, scriptwriter, lead actor, and the whole cast and crew. Ultimately, your whole life is all made up of you, just as all the dreams you've ever dreamt while sleeping have ultimately been made up of nothing but your own creative consciousness. Your creative consciousness produces such a vast array of very realistic scenarios and experiences while your body is resting, and perhaps also when it is awake.

In this view, if there were an accurate credit roll at the end of your life, the credits would have to read, "you, you, you, you, you, you, and you" – not the *little you*, who needs to protect yourself from others, but the *deeper soul you*. Your greatest Self is forever one with everything that exists in this grand universal dance of the one supreme energy of life – this dance of the universal Soul.

Just imagine, our most dramatic "delusions of grandeur" may be but a shimmer of our true greatness. You may think that you're some version of "God's gift to women," when, in fact, you are truly God's gift to His or Her entire creation, and to His and Her very own Self. This kind of elevated awareness can be a great boon in your journey of spiritual happiness, especially if you remember that *everyone else* is also God's great gift to all of creation.

Just as the same rich soil can grow so many types of fruits, vegetables, and grains, so this great field of supreme consciousness has grown all of us. And just as many different ornaments, statues, and pieces of jewelry can be made from the same gold, so everything in this physical universe is made of the same atomic and sub-atomic particles, and ultimately, of the same creative consciousness. The great power of God's Supreme Will vibrates at many frequencies to manifest in and as every physical and non-physical object and creature that exists in this world. With this view of the world as a play of Supreme

Consciousness, you may find it easier to discern and learn whatever lessons your soul is here to experience.

> *Contemplation is that condition of alert passivity, in which the soul lays itself open to the divine Ground within and without, the imminent and transcendent Godhead.*
> **– Aldous Huxley**

Perhaps you were born rich, and you may wonder why destiny would have handed you this experience of easy wealth. You may consider that perhaps your soul is here to learn lessons of humility or generosity in the face of plenty. After all, having great wealth can bring its own challenges to the evolving spiritual soul, such as potential propensities toward pride and callousness.

If you are wondering why you may have had the experience of being poor, you could consider whether that poverty may have been intended to simplify you, to humble you, or to remind you of who you really are. Sometimes the experience of poverty actually makes the outer world so uncomfortable that we'll be much more willing to turn within to touch the divine unknown that exists in the spiritual realms and in our own soul.

Of course, poverty and riches of many kinds come and go in any person's life, so we don't have to limit ourselves to interpreting the deeper meaning of only one particular phase of our lives. Each of us has moved through many phases, from infanthood to wherever we are right now. Some say that we've also had many lifetimes to boot, so that opens up everything for even more vast and creative contemplations in terms of our personal lessons and spiritual evolution.

There can be many possible reasons for any particular circumstance of life, so it's not that you're going to be able to write a thesis that neatly explains exactly why you have experienced every single circumstance. Nevertheless, the practice of exploring and contemplating who you really are definitely adds some interesting dimensions of thought and experience to even an apparently boring or mundane life.

Contemplating the deeper meanings behind outer events makes life more engaging. Even troubles can be enticing if you can see them as being rich in deeper lessons. You may find it helpful to have ongoing discussions within yourself and with other open-minded thinkers to contemplate what lessons may be on your "karmic plate," as well as on the karmic plate for the world at large.

I have found this kind of contemplation to be more potent in improving my life than just running all over trying to fix things without making efforts to decipher some of these deeper reasons and potential lessons behind whatever may feel challenging at any particular time.

Some people come, live, and die, without even *trying* to figure out what it all might be about. Many live lives filled mostly with worldly concerns, such as: How can I get this car? How can I get this job? How can I take care of my children? How can I find the right mate? Such questions may take up their entire sphere of day-to-day thinking, keeping these folks always focused on events they are expecting or fearing in the future, rather than allowing them to be present for every moment of their lives, as is, right here and right now.

In fact, one key to spiritual happiness is to be attentive to each moment. Even if you are thinking about something that may happen in the future, you can train yourself to think about the future while still being focused in the present moment.

Try it right now. Bring in all the tendrils of your attention and focus on this very moment. Look at yourself – your posture, your dress, your current location and environment. Look around. Listen to the sounds going on around you. Watch how you are breathing. Is there a breeze? Are there sounds or activities going on around you? Are there thoughts dwelling in your mind? Are you waiting for something, or hoping for something, or fearing for something? See if you can bring all the petals of your great flower of the mind back into the present moment, just by willing to do it.

From the present moment, think of all the many faces you've worn throughout this life and perhaps other lives, and in this world and perhaps other worlds. Behind all these faces that you've worn, there is a thread. That thread, upon which all your faces and experiences are strung, is your soul. And the divine thread of your soul is also connected with the soul fabric of everything that is known or unknown – weaving through every single person, being, and object that exists.

> *God dwells within you, as you.*
> — **Baba Muktananda**

This personal and universal soul is what the ancient sages from India called *Atman* – the supreme Self. Some who have experienced this Atman have described it as a fountain of a universal happiness that the yoga scriptures call *Ananda*, or supreme bliss.

It is specifically to remember who they are and to enter this realm of supremely blissful Atman Soul that yogis, monastics, and meditators of many cultures and traditions have sat quietly – for minutes a day, for hours a day, or for weeks, months, years, decades, or a lifetime. The practice of meditation can certainly be a helpful support for finding spiritual happiness. It can bring peace, healing, and rejuvenation to body, mind, and spirit.

In the silence of meditation, we rest, aware. We practice being receptive, while surrendering to the purifying energy of nature's healing life force. We tap into the nourishment drip of the great Atman Soul, and receive its rejuvenating fluids into our physical, mental, emotional, and spiritual selves. We settle back into our pure nature.

To remember and honor who we are is the root of our spiritual happiness tree.

❧

Know Your Weakest and Strongest Links

You have been told that, even like a chain, you are as
weak as your weakest link. This is but half the truth.
You are also as strong as your strongest link.
— **Kahlil Gibran**

It's the dichotomy of humanity. On one hand, we human beings can be so good. We are great and divine beings, capable of shining our love, compassion, and wisdom upon the land. As a species, we tend to cheer rescues, mourn losses, and generally like the idea of helping those in need, whether we always actually *do* it or not.

When moved to care, we care with such enthusiasm. When moved to express, we are so creative. When moved to love, we are so selfless. Yet, at the same time, humanity still has so many animalistic tendencies. You and I contain the potential for wreaking all kinds of havoc upon ourselves, others, and the whole planet.

As a species and as individuals, we are both our strongest links and our weakest links, mixed together in a flavorful, bittersweet cup of human nature.

Our strongest links may be clear and caring, brilliant, funny, happy, loving, and a master of exceptional timing – revealing all the best qualities that we admire and would wish to experience in ourselves and in others. On the other hand, our weakest links can be somewhat petty, judgmental, moody, greedy, controlling, self-serving, fearful or angry.

59

Think about your own self. Every one of us carries different varieties and percentages of purity and impurity, good and bad, weak and strong. Each of us is designed with a different recipe and combination of ingredients, including genetics, environment, and many unknown special sauces. We also have individualized taste buds through which we experience the world, and either smack our lips with satisfaction or grimace in distaste.

The conflicting pulls between our higher and lower natures can keep us from experiencing spiritual happiness. In some cases, our stronger self may be feeling guilty for what the weaker self does. At other times, our weaker self may forget what the stronger self knows, and be unhappy due to the dissatisfaction of forgetting our greater nature. The degree of polar oscillations between "pure, good, strong self" and "impure, bad, weak self" varies from person to person. Contemplate yours. Watch your thoughts, speech, and actions. Study yourself. Honor and respect yourself enough to really get to know all the aspects that make up you.

Think about moments when you were going with the flow – being naturally and effortlessly wise, loving, good, kind, skillful, funny, and perhaps even brilliant. These represent the strong links in the chain of who you are. Now think of times when you may have felt jealous, petty, angry, spoiled, or defeated. These are your weaker links.

One helpful application of contemplating our weakest and strongest links is to learn not to take important actions when we're in the weakest link. If something has upset you and your mind is racing, your blood is rushing, your emotions are throbbing, and you find yourself thinking weak, inferior-minded thoughts, consider that this may not be the best time to make that important phone call, to contact a person with whom you're upset, or to go into your boss's office to ask for a raise. Otherwise, you may get some version of, "You *are* the weakest link. Goodbye!"

An awareness of our multi-faceted nature can help us to experience greater spiritual happiness, because it opens the door to integrating the various aspects of ourselves into a more holistic level of self-awareness. To support this integration, we can strive to remain aware of our strongest links, not only when we're feeling strong, but also when we're feeling weak. We can be aware of our weakest links when we're weak and also when we're strong.

Use your intention and remembrance to draw strength from your strongest link when you're feeling weak, and to give guidance and blessings to your weakest link when you're feeling strong.

Being aware of our multi-faceted natures also gives an opportunity to integrate many dichotomies within ourselves, so we can speak and act with clear intentions. For example, sometimes our strongest link will want us to do something wonderful, but our weakest link may self-sabotage our efforts with tactics such as procrastination, shyness, or self-doubt. Understanding our strongest and weakest links is the first step toward healing and uplifting them.

Even though many of our internal dramas and struggles take place below the threshold of our usual awareness – in what psychologists refer to as the subconscious mind – we nevertheless do hold the key to overcoming the weaker self's tendencies. This key exists in the power of our intention. Intention is a major key in shaping our lives from the inside out.

Just by *intending* to expand the best of what exists in you, that very choice will help create more opportunities for expanding and increasing what is best in you. You can live like an artist – painting the landscapes of your life, and uplifting both your weakest links and strongest links into a realm of spiritual awareness, spiritual faith, and spiritual happiness. You'll be your own best friend, the maestro of your life song.

❧

Cultivate Dual Awareness

A seeker once asked the spiritual teacher Poonjaji, "Does enlightenment mean that you are always happy? When you get angry, are you peaceful, happy and blissful inside?"

Poonjaji's response was: "Happiness is permanent. It is always there. What comes and goes is unhappiness. If you identify with what comes and goes, you will be unhappy. If you identify with what is permanent and always there, you are happiness itself. Anger is one of my good friends. He is always there when I need him to transact some business. He is very useful. He does his work without disturbing me and then stays away till I need him again."

Part of this journey of spirituality and spiritual happiness is to train ourselves to look at events more through the uplifting eyes of our clear and powerful spiritual mind, and less through the eyes of those aspects of mind that create turmoil inside ourselves and in the world.

Instead of living mostly in the world of limited appearances, with just a few rare breakthroughs into deeper understanding, we can learn to live in the expanded awareness, viewing the world of appearances from that elevated perception.

This shift into greater awareness is generally a gradual process. It's not so easy to completely turn off one part of your mind and turn on another, except in the rarest stories of beings who underwent massive spiritual enlightenment breakthroughs all at once.

One helpful technique for moving into the elevated perspective is to cultivate a dual awareness. If some event causes your "lower mind" to freak out and respond in ways that are not conducive to spiritual happiness, you don't have to be stuck there alone, without your higher wisdom. You don't have to accept that experience of lower awareness as the *reality du jour*, simply because you are experiencing it in a particular moment. You don't have to wallow in turmoil until you've attained some sort of ultimate enlightenment and become free from all possible negativities. With dual awareness, you can include the blessed vision of your wise soul in your perception and experience of any events, including troubling ones.

With dual awareness, you can watch the same circumstances from two different angles. One eye may be on the nitty-gritty details of a situation, while the other eye sees the supreme consciousness that creates, guides, and exists as the spirit of everything. For example, you can experience and express your opinions about worldly events without being torn apart by gnawing anger or stifling frustrations.

With dual awareness, we can learn to live in this world, while still seeing beyond the illusions of this world. We are *in the world, but not of it.* With dual awareness, we can have the best of both worlds – spiritual and material – rather than always feeling unbalanced on one side or the other.

The practice of dual awareness allows us to respond to events in our lives on the level of those events, even while our awareness is not limited to those levels. Each of us has an individual mixture of personal and karmic ingredients, therefore these various levels and combinations of lower awareness and higher awareness will be unique for each person.

With dual awareness, if someone does something to offend you, you may feel some anger or upset, and may express what you are feeling on an ego-based level of "I can't believe YOU did this to ME!" But then, after – or even while – making your point, you can retreat into the higher spaces of spiritual awareness – whether through meditation or just your own remembrance and intention – and, from there, use the pure energy from that ego-based emotion of anger, fear, or love, to propel you even further into the realm of faith, acceptance, wisdom, and spiritual happiness. With an approach of spiritual awareness, everything becomes grist for the mill of even greater spiritual awareness and spiritual happiness.

This practice of gaining access to our higher vision during challenging times helps us to become more patient, less reactive, and more spiritually happy. Instead of living an aggressive life and getting into brawls with each challenge, we can enter a level of spiritual maturity that keeps us strong and clear, regardless of what does or doesn't come our way.

Ultimately, we may reach a point where there is simply no more room for anger or blame, regardless of what others may have said or done. From an elevated perspective, *everything* is a great gift of life – whether it appears to be pleasant or unpleasant, fair or unfair. The delineations of "good" and "bad" exist only on levels of awareness that are prone to judging, desiring, and fearing, and not on the levels of expanded spiritual awareness.

Of course, a certain amount of judgment is necessary to exist and act in this world. This is where the idea of dual awareness comes in handy. With dual awareness, you can remember your supremely contented inner Self, even while acting in accordance with the outer circumstances of your life. You can use your mind to judge each situation that comes before you, while still maintaining a higher, spiritual flow of awareness.

Deep within yourself, you discover an ever-present flow of blissful, universal divinity expressing perfectly as you, as me, and as everyone else – all together, and all at once. This experience is the foundation of spiritual happiness.

Happiness is a State of Mind

*Your living is determined not so much by what life
brings to you as by the attitude you bring to life; not so
much by what happens to you as by the way your mind
looks at what happens.*
– **John Homer Miller**

The mind is an amazing instrument. When we truly learn to make use
of our mind's potential, it's like having a big power tool that is much
faster, easier, and more efficient than doing the same work just by
hand. We can struggle and struggle through life to barely get by and
make it from one challenge to the next, one disappointment to the
next, and one transitory victory to the next; or we can harness the
tremendous power of our thoughts and intentions to inspire and
empower all of our actions, and to create steady happiness in our lives.

Our minds affect the world around us because thoughts have energy,
and this entire universe is made up of energy. Our minds affect the
world through our thoughts, feelings, and actions, in obvious and
subtle ways. To state it simply: Happy thoughts equal a happy world;
sad thoughts equal a sad world. Fearful thoughts equal a fearsome
world; angry thoughts equal an angry world. Benevolent thoughts
equal a benevolent world; generous thoughts equal a generous world.

What we think literally reflects in the world around us — not just in
some airy-fairy, new-agey way, but because of certain logical, scien-
tific, and philosophical connections that may not be fully described or
studied in today's public school classrooms, but which are nevertheless primary elements of this experience called human life.

I am more and more convinced that our happiness or unhappiness depends more on the way we meet the events of life than on the nature of those events themselves.
—**Alexander Humboldt**

Ultimately, our happiness depends not on what we have, but on how we think and feel about what we have. Although this is an obvious fact of life, few people truly harness the power of their minds to practice intentional happiness.

Once you understand that your mind is the source of happiness, you have an opportunity to consciously take back the reins of your experience of life. You can look at anything that happens, and think, "How can I grow from this? How can I interpret this in a positive way? How can I love, embrace, and make the best of this situation?" You can enjoy the many benefits that come from intelligent, intentional optimism, including the bright and refreshing sun shower of spiritual happiness. With the blessing of your mind, you'll approach life with willingness, inspiration, and joyful ease. Happiness will follow you like a cute little puppy.

☙

Learning to Smile

Start every day off with a smile and get it over with.
– W. C. Fields

Beginning sometime mid-childhood, I developed a habit of walking around with a fairly serious face, even when I was feeling quite fine. I was only marginally aware of this habit until my twenties, while living in an *ashram*, or Indian monastery. My guru noticed my tendency, and hinted about it several times. Once, she mentioned in a letter that it was difficult to see such a serious face all the time. You'd think I would have gotten it from that.

In fact, I did send back a very light and humorous letter to demonstrate my not-so-serious side. My guru's reply to that letter noted that she'd enjoyed its lightness, and suggested that maybe the serious face was "a façade that you like to wear, God knows for what reason."

At the time, I hadn't contemplated this tendency enough to have any real explanation or reason for my often-serious face, although my guru's words did inspire me to take a much closer look at the inner mechanisms involved. Until then, I wasn't even particularly aware of the fact that I looked quite as serious as I did.

First, I considered that, in fact, I *was* fairly serious and determined to make progress on my spiritual evolution while living in this holy, powerful, and fairly intense environment. Yet, I was also having the time of my life, with an abundance of spiritual and creative riches. I was living a life even beyond my dreams come true. I loved the spiritual practices of our monastic life, such as chanting, service, scriptural study, and contemplation, and especially enjoyed having such rich and inspiring outlets for my creative spirit, while creating hundreds of videos about the teachings and events of our spiritual path. I was usually able to fluff petty problems off with my reasonably good sense of humor – which, apparently, only a select few got to see, since I appeared to be "so serious all the time!"

With contemplation, I realized that the serious face truly *was* a façade that I liked to wear, for various reasons that God knew, and that I also wanted to uncover. If I could discover my deeper reasons for choosing to look serious, then I could decide whether I was making the best choice.

The main reason basically boiled down to not wanting people to notice me or to feel jealous of me, especially when I was feeling blessed and happy. I had observed, from a young age, that certain people respond to a happy face by feeling jealous. They might wonder what you'd received that they hadn't, and perhaps would even consider ways to take your blessings away from you. Some people might like to see what your happy face would look like with a frown instead. It's one of those deep, dark corners of human nature – to see someone who has what we might want, and, instead of creating the same for ourselves, to try and take it away from the other person.

In this way, I was contemplating my guru's suggestion that the serious face must be a façade that I liked to wear, for some reason. Nevertheless, I continued to keep my facial muscles more or less in their comfortable, familiar, and not so expressive positions.

Eventually, my guru took the situation to a whole new level, and gave me an instruction that, "you should smile all the time." Several friends also knew about this instruction, and would flash big reminder smiles when we passed in the hallway.

At first, it wasn't too hard for me to smile, since things were actually going pretty well in my life at the time. I was already smiling inside; therefore adding an outer smile was easily doable, although my face *was* aching a bit from the unfamiliar position.

Then came part two of the lesson. All of a sudden, certain situations came about that challenged my happiness. These were fairly minor incidents, but the kinds of things that can be particularly irritating and disturbing. These challenges caused me to feel somewhat upset and most definitely *not* like smiling.

But "smile all the time" was a command from my beloved guru, whose guidance I greatly trusted. I knew that somehow this effort was going to be good for me, even though I wouldn't have chosen to do it on my own. Talk about a struggle of the will – to smile when I wasn't even feeling happy! Yet, what a great way it was to learn to find happiness even during upsetting times.

The only way I could honestly fulfill this command was to actually make myself feel happy enough to smile. If I had tried to smile while upset or angry, that smile would have been more of an insincere grimace (and we've all seen those!), which would not have been honoring the spirit of this directive. And don't think it escaped me to consider that "smile all the time" would also apply to the inner smile!

I had no choice but to find happiness inside myself. Of course, this shouldn't have been so hard, because I still had much to be happy about, in spite of those few irritations that had popped up. Nevertheless, no matter how many great blessings we have, human nature seems to have an engrained tendency to focus a disproportionate amount of our attention on relatively small troubles that may have come along with our wondrous blessings – complaining and getting stuck again and again on the thorns that come along with our beautiful and fragrant roses of life.

Here I was, having been given a command that called me to let go of this tendency to look at troubles more than blessings. I had to choose happiness and deflect unhappiness from my mind. Then, I would be able to offer a sincere smile. Certainly, I did have reasons to be upset, yet my commission was to not let that upset take over my mind. I couldn't, because I had to smile – *all the time*!

In fact, two decades later, when I was asked to write this book on spiritual happiness after having just gone through a particularly challenging seven years, it didn't take long for me to see the hand of my universal guide behind it. This project felt very much like a continuation and expansion of the lesson to "smile all the time." I could almost hear my guru saying, "Okay, now you've been through seven years of illness, poverty, and betrayal by those for whom you have cared and helped the most – now, write an honest and powerful book about happiness!"

Working on this project also brought great blessings, including a new appreciation for the troubling times I'd experienced. With a closer look, those seven years of trial and tribulation were filled with amazing grace and great reasons to be truly, spiritually happy. With contemplative hindsight, I could see that the challenges I had been through would also bring me to write about a deeper level of happiness than just how to "get what you want." After all, what is the use of writing about some temporary happiness that comes and goes depending on uncontrollable outer situations? What we need, and what the world needs, is to find independent happiness, expanded happiness, elevated happiness, and spiritual happiness.

With about six months to write this book, the first two were spent grumbling a bit in my conversations with God. "So, what, now I'm supposed to be happy all the time?" I mean, you'd think I'd be happy that God would want me to be happy, but it's also amazing to see what little doubts and resistances can be hidden when it really comes down to making those big leaps of consciousness, such as the shift into realizing and accepting our own spiritual happiness.

I've chosen to share this experience with you so that you can also recognize any similar resistances that may come up as you move forward on your own journey of spiritual happiness.

Once again, I had to rise up to the occasion and make myself clear and spiritually happy enough to follow *this* command, and to share something worthwhile in this book. It was a similar inner experience to receiving the command to "smile all the time."

Even while going through various layers of inner resistance about becoming a "happiness author," my deep soul smile became bigger and brighter by the moment. What a blessing it has been to focus my mind, heart, and soul on the topic of happiness, and specifically, spiritual happiness. What a gift. I could almost hear God saying, "I want you to be happy," and it was one of the sweetest things I've ever heard inside of myself. I hope that this gift also becomes *your* gift, as you recognize, contemplate, and strengthen your own spiritual happiness.

Happiness is your birthright, and you can uncover that happiness through intention and practice. Intend to be happy, and practice being happy. Imagine that God has spoken inside of you, saying, "I want you to be happy." Feel the freedom that comes from trusting that God wants you to be happy. Give it a go – smile all the time, or at least smile for a while.

Neuroscientists have discovered that using our facial muscles to smile actually feeds back into our brains to spark greater sensations of happiness. So smile, smile, smile. Smile gently, and smile broadly. Smile inside, and smile outside. Let's fill the world with smiling faces, in spite of all the thorns that we could be upset or worried about. Even while acknowledging and striving to fix the problems in our lives and in the world, we can still hold on to our deep sense of spiritual happiness and make a conscious effort to share that happiness with the world.

Play the Game of Life with Empowerment

Positive thinking will let you do everything better than
negative thinking will.
– Zig Ziglar

One of my earliest demonstrations of the connection between my state of mind and the outer world came during my teenage years, when I enjoyed playing on pinball machines, and could usually play a pretty good game. (For you young ones, pinball machines were the predecessors of video games)

While playing, sometimes for hours on end, I'd occasionally notice an uncanny connection between my state of mind and the mechanics of the pinball machine.

Every now and then, I would step up to the machine in a flustered or disconnected state of mind. Maybe I was worried about something, feeling out of sorts, or grumbling in my mind about one thing or another. I'd put the quarter in, and each ball would shoot right down the middle and out the gutter, without giving me even the slightest chance of reaching the ball with either flipper. A hopeless pinball like that is a rare event, but there were times when it would happen to all 5 balls in a row – as though that particular game was unshakably destined to be lost. It was as though an angry "pinball god" was blocking the flow of "pinball grace."

I noticed that these losing games tended to happen when I was in a negative or worried state of mind, and wondered why that might be the case. After all, it's when you're feeling down that you could really use a good game to cheer you up. But the opposite seemed to be the case.

Then, there were times when a different kind of shift would happen. I'd begin to play with a relaxed and peaceful state of mind, with a sense of contentment, and an empowering feeling of trust in my heart. Through that magical porthole of peaceful contentment, I would become free from what I'd later come to know of as *ego* – the aspect of our self-identification that is the source of unwanted feelings such as worry, anger, greed, pride, and fear. Ego is the opposite of true faith. The ego always wants to protect itself, and that frame of mind takes us out of the flow. Since faith is a main key for spiritual happiness, ego can definitely be an obstacle to achieving that happiness. Ego makes every ball go down the middle; freedom from ego creates a stupendous winning game.

While playing pinball in a state of relaxed contentment, it would sometimes seem as though the hands of pleased gods were directing the path of that little silver ball. Effortlessly, I'd watch, as the ball leapt into all the best and most valuable twists, turns, nooks, and crannies of the pinball machine. Bell after bell and melody after melody would chime out to dramatically announce all the new combinations that were racking up points up faster than the machine could even keep up with. I'd hear this symphony of pinball glorification, punctuated by loud clicks as the machine registered newly won free games.

I would be focused and relaxed at the same time, watching with selflessness, enjoyment, and a happy spirit, as an almost magical display of action took place before me. These accomplishments were apparently coming from my own hands and mind, but were obviously being orchestrated by something far beyond my own apparent abilities.

Sometimes, the ball would eagerly dash around, amassing hundreds of thousands of points, without even coming anywhere near my flippers. And when it did come near the bottom of the machine, my fingers would effortlessly and masterfully flip the flippers at just the right moment, and with just the right force to send things back into powerball mode.

You can also apply this teaching to *your* game of life, considering the pinball as a metaphor for your ball of creative effort. One way to improve your game is to increase your level of practice and skill. However, the best help comes from what appears as grace. And, in fact, it *is* grace.

Grace is the magical wild card in this game of life. Grace saves us just when everything appears ready to crumble. With a touch of grace, even our smallest efforts bear great fruit.

Although grace often appears to fall upon us for no apparent reason, there *are* ways to draw grace toward us – by our thoughts and actions, and with an inner state of surrender to the divine, in whatever form that may take for each one of us.

One important task on the quest for spiritual happiness is to discover how our thoughts and actions are manifesting to bring us either happiness or unhappiness, despair or joy, and struggle or ease. This is a research project that each of us must perform on our own, in the laboratories of our own minds, actions, and experiences.

Many books are available to give hints, information, and inspiration on our journeys of discovery. Nevertheless, you ultimately have to discover your own power in your own way. Just as you have to take your own physical exam and your own driving test – no matter how many servants you may have who would be willing to take them for you – in the same way, your spiritual happiness is ultimately your task alone, although supported and nourished by the blessings and grace of many known and unknown great ones from past, present, future, and the *eternal now*.

Part of becoming strong enough to handle a great amount of personal power is to have to go through the lessons and growth of watching and learning for yourself. It's like how a butterfly must struggle against the cocoon in order to develop the wing strength to fly. If someone tries to be helpful by opening the cocoon, the butterfly will not be able to fly.

Don't worry if your journey brings some struggles and strife. Don't worry if the road sometimes doesn't seem to make much sense. Don't fear that you will never be worthy. You are already inherently worthy in your deepest essence. This is the Amazing Grace that saves every so-called "wretch" like you and me. Play your game with love and joy, and trust in that Amazing Grace.

Great Faith Brings Great Freedom

Every tomorrow has two handles. We can take hold of it with the handle of anxiety or the handle of faith.
– **Henry Ward Beecher**

As I mentioned in the first section of this book, if I had to use one word to describe what the essence of spiritual happiness is, at least in terms of my personal experience, that word would be *faith*. Faith can take so many forms. I've had my faith tested by small incidents and large incidents, and have also had my faith justified by small and large demonstrations.

If you think that faith is only justified when you wish for something and it appears before you, well, that may not be quite so – especially if your desires are not yet in harmony with your deeper desires, with the Greater Will, or with the flow of nature. Faith is not just a tool to use for getting what you want, although the ultimate result of faith can be to first learn to want what you get and, from *that* position, to get what you want.

Everyone has different levels and configurations of faith. We may have faith in our families, faith in God, faith in our friends, our abilities, or our inner realizations. We may have faith that the sun will rise tomorrow, or that *those in charge* will make sure we are safe. We may have faith that if something is on the grocery shelf, that means somebody has made sure it is not harmful to our health. Some of our faithfulness is world-based, some is emotion-based, and some is spirituality-based. Some of our faithfulness is strong and directed toward what can truly be trusted, and some is as fragile and delicate as crystals of early morning frost formed on a cobweb under the porch awning in the face of a rising sun.

If someone pursues the practice of faith with extraordinary discipline, diligence and fortitude, they may eventually come to a place of absolute inner freedom. Such was the case with Papa Ramdas, a wonderful spiritual being who lived in India during the 20th century. He wrote many inspired books, and established a monastic ashram in South India that continues to serve many seekers.

Papa Ramdas found supreme happiness through deep faith and trust in God. He came to see every single person as but another face of his beloved God, whom he called "Ram" ("Ramdas" means servant of Ram). Here is a story about how Papa Ramdas responded to a situation that might have brought unhappiness to most people. It involves a thief who came to Ramdas's cave, intending to steal all of his belongings:

> Once Papa Ramdas was dwelling in a cave near a town. As people became aware of his presence they started visiting him and spending time with him. The childlike simplicity and deep devotion with which Papa Ramdas lovingly rendered vibrant spiritual wisdom and stories soon endeared him to the hearts of the people.
>
> Seeing him living without possessions in a bare cave, the local townsfolk started bringing whatever they deemed necessary for his comforts. Soon a cot, a bed, plates, and many other articles were collected in the cave.
>
> The devotees would often visit Papa Ramdas during the daytime, but they left for their homes when darkness descended, and thus Papa Ramdas would remain alone overnight.
>
> Presently, a thief came to know about all the valuables kept in the cave, and one night, after all had left and Papa Ramdas sat alone lost in deep meditation, the thief made his way to the dwelling and ordered Ramdas to collect all his possessions and tie them up in his bed sheet.
>
> To the thief's puzzlement, the saintly man showed no sign of distress. Sunk in divine bliss, Ramdas started packing, and affectionately handed the bundle to the thief with a benign smile. Taking the cot under one arm and the bundle on one shoulder, the rogue walked off and Ramdas sat down on the stony floor, going back into deep contemplation on his beloved Lord.
>
> When morning dawned, the devotees arrived, and were shocked to find an ever-blissful Ramdas sitting in a bare

cave stripped of all possessions. "Papaji", they asked, "Where have all the things gone that were here yesterday?"

Papa Ramdas laughed: "Ram took them away."
The devotees were intrigued: "Which Ram, Papaji?"

"Which Ram? There is only one Ram. Ram gave them and Ram took them away." The saint laughed heartily.

It was only then that they realized the greatness of the sage before them. His serene peace and total absence of regret for all that was gone taught them how free man is when he tears the shackles of attachment.

I first heard this story several years ago, and it has been helpful in continuing to transform and uplift my own experience of faith and inner freedom. Hopefully you'll also be able to take the essence of this lesson to heart. It's not about letting others take advantage of you, but of finding the space of faith and trust within yourself. Have faith that everything is fine – right here, right now, and always – regardless of whether God is giving or taking, and through whom God may be giving or taking.

Trusting God is the greatest clothing you can ever wear. No material possession can match the value of even one iota of faith. As Jesus has said, "If you have faith as small as a mustard seed, you can say to this mountain, 'move from here to there,' and it will move. Nothing will be impossible for you."

Of course, by the time you get to this level of faith, you also attain enough wisdom to keep you from using that power of faith indiscriminately. You wouldn't want to have the power to move mountains, and then casually toss out one curse or another toward a car that cuts you off in traffic! For example, Papa Ramdas did not use his power to harm or even stop the thief, but to strengthen and affirm his own faith and spiritual vision, and to provide a good lesson to the townspeople and all of us, by seeing even the thief as a manifestation of that one, divine being, whom he called "Ram."

> *Cheer up! Cheer up! The case of every one of us is entirely in the hands of God. His will be done! Death and birth are only passing phases in the journey of the soul to Immortality.*
> – Swami Ramdas

Learning to let go of things when they go and welcome whatever comes is a great path for attaining the gem of unshakeable faith in God. This doesn't mean that you have to stop acting with intentions and goals. Nevertheless, once you've surrendered to being in harmony with the Will of God, your actions begin to come from an entirely different place. Although there may be moments of decision, concern, striving, and perseverance, these moments are resting in a grand blanket of faith and trust.

Deep faith allows us to reduce our desires, worries, and attachments to material things. We slough off the clouds that cover our natural, brightly shining, inner soul nature. This story about Papa Ramdas illustrates what this kind of faith looks like in action.

☙

Count Your Blessings

> *If the only prayer you said in your whole life was, "thank you," that would suffice.*
> –Meister Eckhart

Count your blessings, every one of them. Count and relish all your big and small blessings. You know that great feeling of contemplating what you're thankful for on Thanksgiving (in the U.S.), or of praising

God during other Holidays? Well, thanking God is free, and not limited to any country or to any particular day of the year.

Make every day Thanksgiving Day. When you wake up in the morning, open your eyes and thank God for whatever you see before you. As you step into each moment, allow your heart to leap with "Thank you God." Gratitude is the inner blessing that also waters all our flowers of outer blessings.

One reason many don't recognize or appreciate their blessings is because we human beings have certain engrained psychological tendencies toward comparison and relativity. These tendencies seem to be inherent in the wiring of our brains. Many of us have a tendency to judge what we have by comparing it with what others have — most often with those who have more than we do. We get stuck in comparing this with that, me with you, him with her, this job with that job, this car with that car, this career with that one, and this family with that family. I'm sure that every unique person has his or her own list of comparison-minded tendencies.

By observing children, we can see that this tendency can enter the picture quite early, as these young ones clamor and cry to get a toy just because another child has one. The good news is that our tendencies toward comparison and jealousy can be healed and replaced, at least to a great degree, with other qualities from the palette of human colors – such as freedom, service, inner strength, gratitude, generosity, and profound contentment. One of the best steps we can take toward freeing ourselves from these comparison-based causes of unhappiness is to always count our blessings.

Learn to focus on your blessings, regardless of whether others have more or less than you. If you want to turn around a habit of comparing yourself to those who have more than you do, you may want to start by first comparing yourself to those who have less than you do. This can help bring you into a greater sense of gratitude and peacefulness about your own lot. Then you can eventually move into a view of life that stops comparing altogether, and simply be grateful as a natural way of life.

Imagine that your entire life is a big, personally designed, packaged gift from God. Maybe you have a lot of fun toys in your gift, or maybe some bits of challenging coal here and there. Maybe the percentages of toys to coal really do depend on whether you've been naughty or nice in the past, or perhaps it's just the luck of the draw. Maybe some items that appear as lumps of coal are really the best gifts, and vice versa.

Regardless of how many blessings you are able to count in your life, the truth is that if you are able to read or hear this book, then you already have much to be thankful for. If you have education, along with freedom of thought, speech, and religion, if you have shelter and enough food to eat for the next several days, then you are far more blessed than many who live right here, on our planet, today.

Regardless of all that we have, unless we find independent contentment inside ourselves, we may discover that more and more outer blessings will never be enough. Without steady gratitude and contentment, we may receive one outer blessing, then as soon as the excitement of that wears off, we'll need to create yet another blast of relative happiness, again and again.

People can become hooked on this cycle to the point where the ante of outer pleasures has to continuously be upped just to achieve a few small morsels of peace and contentment. Like a drug, they may need more and more dosage of outer blessings just to get the same, temporary experience of happiness. Gratitude, on the other hand, releases an ever-fresh stream of unending contentment and spiritual happiness.

There's Always Good News

Sometimes I think war is God's way of teaching us geography.
—Paul Rodriguez

One quality of spiritual happiness is to know and trust that, somehow, there is always some good that can be found in any situation.

Once a man went to a highly regarded astrologer to find out what was in store for his future. The astrologer told the man, "Well, I have good news and bad news. Which do you want to hear first?"

The man was concerned mostly about what the challenges would be, and requested, "Please tell me the bad news first."

"You have thirty years of misery ahead of you," the astrologer said. "Things are going to crumble and fall apart, left and right."

The man was shocked, but still hopeful. "Well then, what is the good news?"

The astrologer responded, "You'll get used to it!"

Truthfully, there is always a way to look at anything with an eye toward finding blessings there. After all, getting used to having things fall apart may even end up teaching you a detachment that will help you to put *better* things together in the future!

०३

Choose Happiness

We hold these truths to be self-evident, that all men are created equal, that they are endowed by their Creator with certain unalienable rights, that among these are life, liberty, and the pursuit of happiness.
– **United States Declaration of Independence**

The builders of the United States declared that every person has a God-given right to pursue happiness. What a concept that must have been back in their times of hardship and sacrifice. However, being given the right to *pursue* happiness is still a big step away from finding and *attaining* that happiness. As Benjamin Franklin also said, "The U.S. Constitution doesn't guarantee happiness, only the pursuit of it. You have to catch up with it yourself."

Indeed, happiness is a choice for each one of us to make, regardless of what blessings and tragedies have fallen upon our plate of life.

Choosing happiness helps us to think good thoughts, and thinking good thoughts helps to create even more happiness. Instead of waiting for all your desires to be met before you can feel happy, just choose to be happy right now – as is. Simply decide, "I am going to be happy," regardless. Then, even if you're going through some discomforts or troubling times, you'll find that spiritual happiness remains alive like a fresh stream flowing within you.

If you are focused only on your temporary feelings – always asking yourself whether this thing or that person is making you feel happy in each moment – then you'll spend your life at the mercy of outer events that may not always be under your control. On the other hand, if you *choose* to be happy, your experience of happiness is back in your court. Say out loud, "I choose to be happy, right here and right now." Say it, and mean it.

Choosing to be happy doesn't mean that you stop making efforts to improve your circumstances, but that you stop making them with stress and doubtfulness. With a happy spirit, pursue your goals with your best efforts. Choose to be happy, and universal grace may even find ways to surprise you with blessings far beyond your imagined goals. By choosing happiness, you'll be more likely to take clear-headed and clear-hearted actions that can also help to bring your outer life into greater harmony with your essential nature.

With faith and trust, allow the universal power of grace to flow through your life. Don't block that grace with fears, worries, or doubts. Watch your life with happy eyes, and you'll find a happy life.

When one goal manifests, don't be upset thinking, "Where is the other one?" Just be grateful that one has manifested, and let the positive energy of your gratitude feed back into the universe and create even more positive results.

> *Be content with what you have; rejoice in the way*
> *things are. When you realize that nothing is lacking,*
> *the whole world belongs to you!*
> – Lao Tzu

It is ultimately your decision to choose happiness. Why not choose to focus on what is good in life? Appreciate the fact that maybe you did find a pretty good place to live for now. Or maybe you found a job that is not exactly in the location you planned, or in the field you thought, or in the pay range you wanted, but instead of complaining, you say "Yes" to God. "Yes, I will look at the positive things that have come. I trust you, and I trust the universal perfection that expresses fully in my life. I trust that whatever else is meant to come of my goals will come at the right time, with the nourishment of my clarity, faith, and right effort. I choose to be happy – right here, and right now!"

Instead of waiting for something to make you happy, you can choose to feel joy about anything. Right now, there is something in your life that you can feel joy about. Just by feeling that joy, you will be putting out more "joy energy" into your world, and that same joy will reflect and come back to you even more abundantly.

03

If You're Going to Do Something, Do it Cheerfully

My grandfather once told me that there were two kinds of people: those who do the work and those who take the credit. He told me to try to be in the first group; there was much less competition.
–Indira Gandhi

Recently, a friend and I took a walk on "Dog Beach" in San Diego with his dog. As we walked, Kevin stopped to pick up some droppings that had been left by another owner's dog, and mentioned how it has always seemed to be his lot to pick up dog doo – not only from his own dogs, but from others as well. Some residents in the place where he lived apparently would let their dogs go anywhere on the grounds, without picking up the droppings. Kevin, on the other hand, has a very neat and responsible nature, and carries a special pouch of plastic bags with him during doggie walks, specifically for that purpose.

As Jerry Seinfeld once said, any alien watching from above would have to assume that dogs were the intelligent ones, with human beings acting as doting servants, picking up after them whenever they happen to want to relieve themselves.

As we walked, Kevin was kind of complaining about always having to pick up after others. I could clearly see how this attitude made no sense. Of course, it is much easier for us to see such things in others than in ourselves. My response was, "If you're going to do it, then you might as well do it cheerfully."

This idea is something I've contemplated quite a bit in my own life. There is a time for making a decision of whether or not to do something. During that time, you can weigh all your thoughts and feelings about that particular action. However, once you've decided to do something and are doing it, then the best approach is to do it with the most positive interpretation and feeling that you can create. Act with wholeheartedness. Give your full blessings to whatever you do.

> *Approach the present with your heart's consent. Make*
> *it a blessed event.*
> **– Gurumayi Chidvilasananda**

I mean, you're already doing it. Once the decision is made that you're going to do something, then you have two choices: do it bitterly and with a series of complaints, or do it joyfully and with a happy spirit. I suggested that Kevin could even consider this task as a symbolic blessing — for example, he may be paying back some "karmic dues" for times when others may have had to clean up *his* messes in the past. Or maybe each good act of helping to keep our earth clean will add one more good merit feather to his cap, or to the overall good of humanity. With metaphors like this, each pile of doo becomes one more opportunity to pay *our* "dues," to invoke grace, and to serve the world.

Once we discussed these ideas, Kevin realized that he didn't even really mind picking up the doggie messes, and that it had really been comments by others that had made him feel that he'd been taken advantage of by these negligent dog owners. This is another important element for all of us to look at in how we approach what we are doing. Are we allowing the opinions of others to cause us to act with negativity or resentment?

Since we don't fully know how everything in this universe works, why not find positive interpretations for whatever we do and whatever we experience? If we decide to offer help to someone – whether a homeless person on the street, or a friend or relative in need – then let's give whatever we choose to give with love and cheerfulness.

When the Holy One loves a man, He sends him a
present in the shape of a poor man, so that he should
perform some good deed to him, through the merit of
which he may draw to himself a cord of grace.
– **Zohar**

If there are concerns about whether your assistance is ultimately helping or weakening a person, the time to contemplate that is before you give. Once you've decided to give, give with a clean and enthusiastic heart.

This approach of doing whatever we do wholeheartedly is applicable to everything we do, and is likely to bring great spiritual happiness into our lives.

☙

Be Aware of the Words You Use

Some people speak like animals; their words have no
meaning. They chatter day and night like frogs in a
well. People have their own ways of talking, and they
are all different. You should think carefully before you
speak. Words should be uttered with great discrimina-
tion.
– **Sundardas**

One of the key secrets of spiritual happiness is to be aware and careful about the words we use. Words are the currency through which thoughts take form in our minds, and with which they are expressed outwardly.

You can think of choosing your words as though you are selecting the ingredients and flavors for the recipe of your life. God's creative power weaves all of your thoughts and words, along with the thoughts and words of those around you, to create the grand banquet of your life, and together, our collective lives.

Most of today's social and educational systems don't really teach how important words are in creating our lives and the world. I wish they would. Sometimes, when I hear politicians and media personalities using phrases that serve only to defeat their own goals, or our greater goals, I wish I could whisper to them through the screen. "Hey, don't use the words 'evil' and 'evildoers' five times in the same sentence. Pssssst. . . Repeating over and over that, 'They hate us and want to destroy us' is not a good *mantra* or power phrase, nor are big, dramatic television banners saying things like 'Attack on America!'"

Anyone who understood the power of words would be more careful to avoid unintentionally attacking his or her own country with written or spoken words. Nobody who truly understands the nature and power of words would say or print such recklessly negative things – especially not over and over again.

With repetition, our words become even stronger and more engrained in the consciousness of ourselves, of those who are receiving our words, and perhaps into the planetary web of consciousness as well. Words are powerful currencies that deserve great respect and care.

During our daily lives, we may also be programming ourselves for unhappiness through the words and phrases we use. This is especially so for phrases and words that have become a habit. If something goes wrong and you tell the universe – or God no less – to "damn it," well then, who do you have to blame if things get worse instead of better? If you have a habit of saying that people or situations make you sick, then don't be surprised if you end up making substantial use of that HMO insurance plan!

> *For what goes into your mouth will not defile you; but*
> *what comes out of your mouth, that is what will defile you.*
> – Jesus Christ

In a way, we're all like magicians – knowingly or unknowingly reciting mantras, hexes, blessings, and other potent and magical words every time we speak. Some ancient philosophical scriptures explain that the entire world as we know it is created by words. In Sanskrit, the term for this creative energy that expresses through syllables and words to create the universe is *Matrika Shakti,* the Mother Power. Therefore, respect this awesome power of words, and attend to how you're spending the currency of your words with at least as much care as you watch your financial spending.

Of course, it is fine to use words to discuss your burdens with friends, but also remember that every time you put your troubles into word form, you may be solidifying them that much more. See if you can phrase your words in more constructive and positive ways. Catch yourself while speaking, and ask if the benefit of sharing your troubles in word form is worth giving more power to those troubles. Sometimes it is, and sometimes it isn't. As with most things in life, it's a balance.

One method that is always available for uplifting the words in our minds is to intentionally think good thoughts. Whenever you can, replace harmful thoughts with positive thoughts. This is the alchemy behind using positive affirmations to change your life. Do your best to speak and think happy, uplifting, and positive words, and you may find yourself living a more happy, uplifting, and positive life.

Today is the day of my amazing good fortune.
– **Florence Scovel Shinn**

One common way for questionable words to slip into our minds and speech is from hearing and singing songs from the radio or television. Some songs may express ideas and phrases that do not even come close to how we would really like to speak to ourselves or to the universe. And yet, when we sing along, we may even try to match the singer's dramatic delivery and sing as though we are really feeling the emotions being expressed in the song.

Singing with feeling is great if the song has a positive flavor, but may not be so good if the words are describing situations of despair, defeat, and dejection. I've caught myself doing this many times, hearing songs and wanting to sing along. Since I do understand the power of words, I tend to catch myself and stop singing songs that have negative words. Sometimes I'll even make up my own, more positive words so I can still sing along to the tune.

Of course, if you do have some deep despair and sadness, a somber song can be just the medicine for helping you to express and release those feelings. Taking care of the words we use is not about squelching all negative-sounding thoughts and feelings that come up. The hints that I'm sharing are not intended to be made into rigid rules, but are offered to share with you some information and insights that I've found helpful on my own journey. My hope is that these ideas will assist you in orchestrating the words that you hear and speak with a greater awareness of their significance and creative power. This awareness of the power of words can be an excellent tool for creating and supporting your spiritual happiness.

The powerful effects of words can be described either in psychological or spiritual terms. On a psychological level, every single word we speak and every single word we hear goes into our subconscious minds and creates some small or large effect there. How these words affect our psyches and attitudes are inevitably going to have a powerful effect on how we experience, interpret, and respond to the events of life.

On a spiritual level, our subconscious minds are also reflections and facets of the Great Universal Mind of God. Whatever words you input into your personal mind are also being fed into the Great Universal Mind that creates all the circumstances of your life, including your experience of spiritual happiness.

It is for the purpose of gaining control over this immense power behind words that monks of various traditions undergo periods of deep silence. Can you imagine not speaking for 24 hours, much less for weeks, months, or even years? Let me tell you a story about one monk's journey into silence:

Once, an aspiring spiritual seeker wanted to devote his life to God. He went to a monastery, where the head monk told him: "You can stay here, but we have one important rule. All monks must observe a strict vow of silence. You will only be allowed to speak one sentence every twelve years."

The seeker agreed to this austere condition, and spent the next twelve years in complete silence, steeped in prayer, meditation, study, and service.

The day came when it was time for the monk to speak his one sentence. Meeting with the head monk, the young monk said: "The bed is too hard."

After twelve more years of austere discipline, the monk had another opportunity to speak to the head monk. He said: "The food is not good."

Twelve more years of hard work went by, and the now much older monk finally got to speak again. The monk's words after thirty-six years of practice were: "I quit."

The head monk quickly answered: "Well, I'm not surprised. All you have done is complain since you got here!"

CB

Positive Communications Bring Greater Happiness

Happiness is when what you think, what you say, and what you do are in harmony.
–Mohandas Gandhi

Many of us have been brought up being taught to squelch our honest communications for the sake of politeness or political correctness. I suspect that this common tendency of holding back on expressing exactly what we really think is part of what makes the viewing public so enthralled with watching acerbic, insulting hosts – whether on news shows, game shows, or talent audition shows. It's almost as though their blatant, piercing honesty feels good because it balances out our own frustrated communications. Many of us live with a mountain of unspoken thoughts and feelings that have accumulated throughout our lives.

If we can begin to clear our minds of old angers and resentments that may have been bottled up inside ourselves long ago, we'll be better able to communicate more clearly to people today. Unprocessed angers and resentments tend to seep through what we say, even to those who may have had nothing to do with the original offences. It's like the idea that someone may have had a bad day at work and come home and kick the dog, so to speak, except that the sources of certain angers and resentments may be very old and deeply embedded in our psyches, and are therefore not so easy to discern.

The more you can keep your mind and heart clear of undigested emotions, the more effective your communications will be. This doesn't mean that you have to be in silence all the time, or only espouse wise sayings all day long – although either of these options is fine if it's your thing. Without the fear of losing yourself in undigested anger and other destructive emotions, you'll be better able to speak up for yourself before things get out of hand. You'll be able to speak honestly and kindly at the same time.

Inevitably, there are going to be people in this world who will try to take advantage of you, or who will disrespect, harm, or steal from you in some way. This is just part of human life at this particular time of evolution. Not everyone understands that good for one is good for all, and harm to one is harm to all. When you meet such challenging people or obstacles, you'll tend to do much better by communicating, asking questions, or giving honest feedback than you will by holding everything inside and having all your doubts, fears, and angers come out in harmful ways.

A build-up of undigested emotions can create uncontrollable explosions of upset that blast forth after it's too late to communicate honestly but nicely – after you've already lost your happiness and composure, as well as perhaps your relationship and your job. Therefore, it is generally best not to wait for troubles to get out of hand before communicating your thoughts and feelings about them.

When you're not in danger of bursting open from pent up emotions or falling into some uncontrollable rage, then you will also be able to assess problems more clearly and objectively as they arise. In any relationship – whether personal, business, or otherwise – you can communicate your feedback when someone has pushed one or two of your buttons, instead of waiting until they've pushed ten. Even if someone doesn't like hearing what you have to say, you'll be able to share your honest thoughts more gently *before* things get out of hand, than after they've gotten worse. By being truthful and speaking with clarity, you'll be honoring yourself as well as the other person.

Maybe you're concerned that if you speak your truth, someone might become angry and take something away from you, such as their friendship or assistance. However, if you can get to a place where you trust God, trust yourself, and trust the other person's soul – which is also a spark of the Universal Soul – then you can learn to say things clearly, quickly, and in a way that's easier for another person to receive, without waiting until things get out of hand. Your life will become smoother and clearer in the long run, and you'll have self-respect, which is worth more than any friendship or business deal that would fall apart simply because you're being honest about what you think and feel.

Of course, there is always a need for balance between giving positive, honest feedback, and just complaining all the time. Many of us choose to not communicate our thoughts because we don't want to come off as obnoxious complainers. It took me a long time to learn how to speak my mind in the right way and at the right time. I'd often remain silent, even in the face of injustice. In fact, this was one of the important lessons that I encountered while living in an ashram, with the guidance of my spiritual guide, or guru.

In one lesson, my guru had called me into her meeting room to ask about some false accusations that had been made about me. I was working as video editor for the spiritual organization at that time, and the apparent accusations were that I'd erased precious video footage from the archives, and that I'd requested that several hundred video-tapes be sent from New York to California, among other similar statements that were not at all accurate or true. Nevertheless, my dear guru mentioned each accusation on the list to me, awaiting my response to each one. I offered very little response in defense, even though the accusations were obviously silly and incorrect.

In fact, I had grown to believe that silence was an appropriate response to most challenging situations. I was also fairly shy, and thought that saying nothing would be preferable to possibly saying the wrong thing. After all, the ability to speak clearly, honestly, and positively can take some practice.

When asked about these untrue aspersions, I barely eked out a response. Obviously, my guru also knew that the accusations weren't true, and, after watching my lack of response to them, she commented that, "You never stand up for yourself!"

Now, I didn't quite know if this was a good thing or a bad thing. After all, I always examined the words of my guru with great care and respect. She didn't exactly say, "You *should* stand up for yourself." Perhaps it was just a call for me to contemplate the tendency and become more self-aware about why I wouldn't stand up for myself.

While contemplating my guru's assessment, I realized that, along with whatever shyness or childhood defense mechanisms may have contributed to my tendency to not stand up for myself, another deeper root of my silence came from faith in God. Why should I have to defend myself in God's creation, when everything that exists is made up of one all-knowing divine God consciousness?

I had also read many stories about saints and sages who chose not to descend into the level of "he said, she said," and who strengthened and proved their trust in God by remaining serene in the face of injustice. From such stories, I thought that a good spiritual person should maintain silence in unjust situations.

However, through many years of contemplating my guru's words, I've also come to understand that sometimes silence is a good response, but at other times, speaking up can be helpful for creating greater happiness in life. And, although very few people enjoy receiving criticism, the right critique, offered in the right way and at the right time, may also be exceptionally helpful in giving others the kind of feedback that can help make their lives happier in the long run.

The important thing to do when you're about to give some possibly critical feedback is to scan your mind and emotions. Look inside to see that your intentions are pure. Make sure you're not just wanting to put someone down, or that you're not just expressing your own hardened patterns of opinions and frustrations.

Obviously, anything we do in this world will tend to be a mixed bag of motivations, however one step we can take to purify our motivations before communicating honest feedback to others is to stop for a moment and use our own will power and mental power to observe and ensure that our intentions are anchored in good. Visualize what you hope the outcome of your communication will be. Our intentions are the powers behind our actions; therefore, we should always pay attention to our intentions whenever we act or speak.

Don't wait for things to get so out of hand that you can't control your anger about a person or situation. As soon as things get a little bit bad, you can take action, speak up, and deal with the budding problem right then. Don't wait for a sprout to become a big yard full of tangled weeds.

If you're upset with somebody and don't communicate with them about why you are upset, then they'll most likely continue doing things that rub you the wrong way, and you'll most likely keep bristling and feeling anger. Such emotions could end up affecting your state of mind, your work, your home life, and all kinds of things – including, of course, your experience of happiness.

Of course, balance is also required with learning to communicate honestly and positively. To create *outer* happiness along with *spiritual* happiness, we may need to control our outer expressions to some degree. If you went around indiscriminately telling everyone exactly what you really think, some of those folks may not like you so much anymore. You might push their buttons, or break their rules.

I remember a scene from the black and white, 20th century, "I Love Lucy" television show, where Lucy and her friends, while playing cards together, made a pact to speak exactly what they thought, honestly and fearlessly. Eventually, they critiqued one another's style of dress and behavioral traits to such a degree that, by the end of the card game, they were all quite angry at one another. Therefore, this practice of communicating with clarity and honesty is always a balance, as well as a skill that we can continually cultivate and refine.

> *A diplomat is a person who can tell you to go to hell in*
> *such a way that you actually look forward to the trip.*
> *– Caskie Stinnett*

Some folks might bristle a bit from even well intentioned honesty, but they may also eventually find your honest feedback helpful in their own journeys – perhaps without even realizing that some of their positive shifts were sparked by your honest communications. This is one reason why being helpfully honest requires a certain amount of service mentality and detachment from receiving immediate positive feedback from what you have offered.

What matters most is your intention – your attitude of positive helpfulness. If you are feeling anger toward a person or situation, it would probably be best to first take some time to cool off and contemplate what you'd really like to say, beyond just getting something off your chest. Being "honest" in the name of taking revenge or hurting someone's feelings would not be advised. It could make the outer situation worse, and could also bring some unwanted *karmic* reactions into your life.

The idea of *karma* is, in basic terms, cause and effect. Every action has an equal and opposite reaction. In the most simplistic terms, you could say: good in, good out, and bad in, bad out. The actual science of karma is not nearly as simple and neat as that, however, in general, you can assume that positive actions create positive results, and that negative actions create negative results. Within this model of karmic action and reaction, it is our intentions that come back with the most potency.

If we act with a pure intention of being helpful, our actions are more likely to bear positive fruit. Nevertheless, we don't always need to have obvious positive responses and outcomes to know that we are doing the right thing. We know in our soul when we are coming from a pure intent of helpfulness. That's the best time to communicate. With a clear heart and clear communications, we're able to cut out many potential problems at the root, nipping troubles right in the bud. In this way, we begin to create a more honest and happy life, for ourselves and for those around us.

◌◌

There's Always a Way to Create Happiness

I have become my own version of an optimist. If I can't make it through one door, I'll go through another door - or I'll make a door. Something terrific will come no matter how dark the present.
–Rabindranath Tagore

One of my friends who is a western-born *swami* – a monk of an Indian tradition – recently told a wonderful story. He was spending several months away from his usual monastery while doing some service in Delhi, one of India's larger cities. Swamiji's daily requirements often took him through one particular section of town, where the cars would have to slow down or stop for a while. As the cars moved slowly through the road, a group of young boys would be going from car to car, begging for money. This put my friend in a quandary.

Swamiji is especially attuned to befriending youth, because much of his monastic service has been involved with guiding teens on the spiritual path. He has quite a practical jokester sense of humor, which is just about right for entertaining adolescents. In fact, he's pulled a few practical jokes on me in the past.

Here were these poor, sad-looking beggar children asking for rupees, however, with my friend being a monk, it was not really appropriate for him to give money to the children in that way. At the same time, the swami didn't feel right just ignoring these children when they came to the car window. He was much more used to playing and laughing with children than uncomfortably ignoring them. I'm sure that anyone who has driven or walked through major cities of any country must have experienced the discomfort of not knowing how to respond to beggars on the road.

The swami had recently received a gift from his guru — a funny-looking cat puppet that almost looked real. He had an idea. The next time they drove through that part of town, Swamiji brought the cat puppet along. When one of the kids came by his car to beg for change, Swamiji reached up with the hand puppet on, and grabbed the child's arm. The child looked at the strange creature, squealed, and ran away.

At first, Swamiji was concerned that he had scared the child off, but soon the boy returned with the rest of the children. They all wanted to see the cat puppet, and the next thing you knew, the kids were all laughing and reaching out so the cat puppet could grab them too. From that day on, every time the swami's car came through that area, the boys would run to surround his car and play with the cat puppet. Talk about turning an uncomfortable situation around to create happiness!

This is what spiritually happy people do — they approach common situations with uncommon radiance and heartfelt thoughtfulness. Every person on this planet has had the experience of seeing someone in need that you'd like to help, and perhaps could help in some small way, or on a temporary level. You may not have the means to really help the person, or you may know that helping in that way would only serve to continue the cycle of poverty for them. You're only one little person with limited finances – you can't just pour a few thousand billion dollars into uplifting conditions for those in need around the world. What can one person do?

Perhaps you can still offer a smile, a blessing, or some friendly words. Or you could break out a cat puppet. Ask your heart for guidance on how you can create happiness in any situation, according to your own best nature.

What the swami did was to give these children something even more precious than they would ever have dreamed of finding on that noisy street. Forget the few rupees that they were begging for; the swami helped them to experience happiness, love, playfulness, laughter, and ecstasy. And what did he get back from giving that? More, more, and more of the same. This story is a great illustration of how giving is receiving, and how the light we give to others also reflects back upon ourselves. Happiness shared is happiness multiplied.

The final touch of Swamiji's experience came on the day when he was leaving Delhi. He hadn't told the boys that he was leaving that day, and yet, acts of joyful good will often bring amazing and grace-filled synchronicities — the miracles of life, if you will. As the swami's car made its way through the street on that last day of his stay in Delhi, there were the children. They had been working on their own gift for him. Without even knowing that this was the swami's last day, the children happily surrounded the car, and began singing in English, "We love you, we love you!"

How beautiful life is when we seek and find happy solutions for challenging problems!

CB

Arrange Your Priorities

Every time you wake up, ask yourself, "What good things am I going to do today?" Remember that when the sun goes down at sunset, it will take a part of your life with it.
– **Native American Proverb**

One quick step toward spiritual happiness is to take some time to contemplate and clarify your priorities, and to compare them with where you are spending most of your time, efforts, and money. If most of your resources are going for things that you don't really care so much about, then you can begin to contemplate ways to change that percentage. Choose what areas are most important to you, and focus your attention primarily in those areas. Read about them, think about them, and talk about them – continually clarifying and empowering your interests and areas of greatest priority.

If your children are your greatest priority, then make sure your work load is not keeping you from spending an appropriate amount of time with them — even if that may mean choosing to live a simpler life. If success is your priority, then don't spend all your time with those who have no interest in achieving success, with people who don't believe in your potential, or in social circles that do not support and nourish your goals. If spirituality is your priority, then find a way to make time for spiritual retreats – whether personal retreats at home, or in group gatherings.

What are your priorities in life?

We've all had many experiences of having to rearrange our priorities. Just in the process of growing from a child into an adult, our interests and goals have changed many times. What this secret asks us to do is to put some effort into arranging our priorities consciously – looking to see what they are, putting them in some order of importance, and fixing up any minor priorities that are contradicting or interfering with other, more important priorities.

Taking time to contemplate and arrange your priorities will help you to move forward with a clear vision and intention. You won't have to keep falling into valleys of unhappiness, realizing that you haven't found what you truly want because all of your time and money went toward ambitions that did not fulfill your deepest needs.

Before you get swept away by society's expectations for you, or by your family's and friends' wishes for you, first take some time to really contemplate what in life brings *you* happiness. Delve into the depths of your spirit, and ask your soul what is your mission in life? Look back on your life, from childhood on. What do you most like to do? What gives you the greatest sense of meaning? What are you here to learn? What are you meant to give? What will bring you in tune with your most wonderful nature? What will give you the kind of steady contentment that will remain with you until – and perhaps even beyond – your last breath in this body?

For example, we can consider that many smaller enjoyments of life would be available if we forfeited certain other large expense items, including large houses, fancy cars, and even children. Raising children is certainly a long-term large expense of both time and money – this is an investment that is worthy of contemplation, especially in this time of world over-population.

If you want to have children, houses, or fancy cars, of course, that is absolutely fine. The problem arises when people move only through the grooves of wants and needs that have been set by others, without looking within themselves to find their true priorities and passions in life.

Even while living within the boundaries of common social acceptance in whatever culture you live, you can still contemplate what it is that you want to give to this world, and what you want to receive from this world. This is your life; live it! If your deepest joy comes from climbing mountains, by golly, go find a way to climb some mountains!

> *Time is the coin of life. Only you can determine how it will be spent.*
> – Carl Sandburg

Perhaps your love is longing to express in the care of children – receiving their joy and creative growth in your own life, while offering your love and wisdom into the world to and through them. If so, then please do put your time, efforts, and money into bringing more blessed souls into this world.

But, perhaps you don't really have such a strong maternal or paternal instinct. You may find greater fulfillment in offering your resources in other directions, such as caretaking various aspects of society, or in creating artistic expressions that will touch people's minds, hearts, or souls.

Whatever is your deep inner calling, according to your individual nature, that is where the bulk of your thoughts, efforts, and resources can be best directed.

❧

A Personal Sharing about Shifting Priorities

Get up and dance, get up and smile, get up and drink
to the days that are gone in the shortest while.
– **Simon Fowler**

Here, I'll narrate a personal story about some fairly recent priority shifts that have taken place in my life. The first half of the story illustrates how I consciously rearranged my priorities when necessary, using contemplation and spiritual knowledge to help myself flow and grow with outer changes that had taken place. The second half shows how the hand of grace helped me to remember and realign myself with my deeper priorities, even as that guiding hand came cloaked within some unexpected challenges.

Hopefully, you'll be able to apply some of these lessons to your life. You may even find many more lessons in this story than I discuss here, because it – like most intense life stories – has many layers of potential meanings and lessons. If I were to delve into all the events of the past decade, it would certainly take many more pages than are available here. Therefore, I'll focus mainly on aspects of this story that relate to this one secret of arranging our priorities.

In 1989, I left a decade of monastic life and moved to not-so-monastic Hollywood. For this transition, I had to shift my priorities from austere ones – such as silence, spiritual study, and selfless service – to the kinds of thoughts, actions, and speech that would be conducive to living a successful life in Hollywood. After all, I wanted to be in harmony with my environment, and Hollywood is what was being presented before me at that time. I had just spent a decade living in a monastic ashram, where one of the main teachings was to see the play of God in and as everything. I thought, "Okay, God. You want me to play Hollywood? Fine, I'll play Hollywood!"

I was quickly hired as an editor and producer for a number of popular television shows and media companies. Within the first year or so, I'd edited a *Candid Camera* episode with Alan Funt, edited the brand new tabloid show, *Hard Copy*, put together an interview with Charlie Rose and Bob Hope, and was hired as a full-time editor for Disney's "Prime Nine News" show. Life was certainly looking different from how it looked during my monastic days.

Within a few years, most of my friends were actors, casting directors, or producers. Three years after leaving the monastery, I was spending Thanksgiving evening chatting and drinking peppermint schnapps with Arnold Schwarzenegger, as he puffed on his cigar and told me all about how he'd made different scenes for his various movies. It was actually a little embarrassing, because I hadn't seen any of his movies, having spent so much time in a monastic life!

I also enjoyed meeting and chatting with other celebrities, although the "equal vision" practice of seeing God in everyone did tend to keep me from getting *too* star-struck.

In Hollywood mentality, the goal is generally to move up and make bigger projects with bigger paychecks. One popular t-shirt said "But what I really want to do is direct!" Instead of being fully focused on where they were, most of my Hollywood friends were always looking for the next step up, either by moving to a better position in their current show, or by moving to another. This was part of the dance of Hollywood, land of dreams.

I became somewhat swept up by the expectations of that society, as a whole new set of priorities arose in my life. I tend to be fairly flexible in fitting into any environment – which can be either a blessing or a detriment, depending on the outer circumstances. I did manage to fit fairly well into this new realm of Hollywood mentality, and also got to learn first-hand how easily we can be affected by our environments. My priorities shifted from wanting to be as spiritual and selfless as possible, to being more focused on outer works and accomplishments.

Of course, every experience has its blessings, and I believe that this "Hollywood" shift of priorities was also a great blessing. My experiences in Hollywood gave me a personal confidence and worldly know-how that would allow me to eventually be able to share some of the deep spiritual wisdom that I'd learned in the monastery, in an entertaining and accessible way. As I told the acquisitions editor who hired me to write *Spirituality For Dummies*, "I've lived in the depths of monastic life, and in the depths of worldliness – I can chant like a Brahmin, and cuss like a sailor!"

This is another point I'd like to make about arranging priorities. We don't have to get stuck in any one set of outer priorities and think that we have to stay with them forever. Sometimes we may have lessons that lead us into different scenarios with different priorities. However, without a conscious understanding of ourselves as the arrangers of our own priorities, we may find ourselves swept away into a life that never quite meets our deeper goals. We may lose sight of our soul's priorities, which remain constant beneath and throughout any outer shifts that we may experience.

During these years of Hollywood magic and excitement, I began to notice a deep and growing sense that my efforts toward greater achievement in the film and television business were not really moving me toward the areas of greatest soul priority in my life.

When it is time for us to rearrange our priorities, the clue can often come as a subtle sense of dissatisfaction with what we are doing. Of course, obstacles and dissatisfactions can arise even when we are on the right path, so it is not as simple as saying that challenges mean that you should be giving up or changing your goals and priorities.

One way to check whether you are living in accordance with your deeper priorities is to imagine yourself reaching the pinnacle of your present goals, and to contemplate if that accomplishment would bring you a deep sense of satisfaction. How would it feel to reach the best outcome of wherever you are headed? Would it bring true fulfillment and happiness?

For me, this contemplation happened during that Thanksgiving evening with Arnold Schwarzenegger. I thought, "This must be what it is like at the end of the Hollywood journey – hanging out with other super-famous folks and discussing all of your movies, television shows, and other projects."

Let's say that I moved forward with all my heart and soul and became as creative and successful as someone like Arnold, or Steven Spielberg. Would that give me a sense of fulfilling *my* deepest ambitions and goals? The answer was, no.

I realized that even if I made it to the so-called top of this profession, I would not feel deeply satisfied from that accomplishment. Something was missing in my life, and I could feel it knocking on my heart's door.

I had been swept up by the mentality and priorities of this new social system called Hollywood, and that sweep had kept me too busy to stop and reconsider what was most important in my life. I'm sure this must happen to many people in various fields of life and career. We get too busy and absorbed in the necessities of each day to stop and contemplate why we're even doing all that we are doing.

By 1994, I was working on several jobs at once, helping to create the two hottest children's shows of the time. I bounced back and forth from editing and associate producing the television show *X-Men*, to editing the *Mighty Morphin' Power Rangers* – working however many hours were required to make sure both shows were done well. The work was creative and fun, and the friends I worked with were amusing, although occasionally risqué, and, at times, vulgar. During this phase, I was definitely treated to an entirely new vocabulary of words and concepts that would *not* have been conducive to a pure and peaceful monastic life!

As time went on, I began to feel more and more world-weary. I kept thinking, "I wish I had more time; I just wish I had more time." My schedule was so busy that I needed some time alone, some time to rest. I needed some time to contemplate and digest all the blessings I had received and generated during so many years of dedicated spiritual practice, study, and service. I needed to stop and rearrange my priorities, however, I was just too busy to do so.

I was working up to eighty or even one-hundred hours a week, putting all my precious time into projects that were somewhat fulfilling in a creative sense, but not truly where my heart's desire was leaning. I'm sure that many have felt what I was feeling — a certain satisfaction with success, but also a deep inner questioning of whether this was all I was meant to do with my grand gift of life.

Eventually, my wish for more time came, although in a slightly unexpected way. I became physically ill, and could barely do anything for nearly seven years. I had to quit both of my jobs, and would just sit and sit and sit. I had no idea that the challenge would go on for so long, or that my life would become so simplified by the physical limitations, along with the resultant financial limitations.

Around the same time, an even more challenging scenario emerged. Someone who I'd considered the dearest of friends, and who I'd helped to clarify and achieve her greatest dreams and goals, began to spread untrue rumors about me throughout our spiritual community. We had recently grown apart, and astonishingly, instead of offering the kindness and care that I would have certainly offered to her, my dear old friend was trying to harm my reputation and spirit during my time of illness and poverty. What a surprise that was.

As my friend's untrue rumor spread through our worldwide spiritual "village," it quickly ate away at decades of spiritual friendship and community. Nearly everyone who I had considered as a friend evaporated, like dust. There I was, after ten amazing years of monastic life and seven exciting years of Hollywood life – too physically ill to work, about to enter years of financial poverty, and completely alone in this world.

In the midst of all this, came an inner experience that helped me to approach this new shift with a refreshed sense of enthusiasm and gratitude.

While sitting quietly one day, I remembered my oft-repeated wish for more time. "If I could only have more time. I just need to have some time alone." Ahh, yes. That had been my ongoing wish during all those years in Hollywood.

"I just need to have some time alone." I had been longing for a solitude away from the vibrations of thought, greed, ambition, useless speech, empty relationships, and false facades of communication and mis-communications. And that's just what God had given to me. See? We have to be careful about how we word our wishes! Be specific!

Nevertheless, this realization helped me to see the unfolding events with a dual perspective. Along with plugging away through the day-to-day challenges, I also realized that I'd been given exactly what I'd asked for. I now had day after day of precious, peaceful, quiet time for relishing the blissful comfort of being completely alone.

The recognition of this new set of life circumstances as a gift from God shifted my approach. I wanted to make good use of this gift. Instead of just wallowing in misery or self-pity, I used this time and these circumstances to reconnect with my deeper spiritual wisdom. From there, I began, once again, to arrange and rearrange my priorities.

First, I looked at my physical situation. With a growing list of troubling and painful ailments, I considered that this failing health might possibly be leading to my time of leaving this world.

I was feeling more or less at peace with that possibility, when, in the midst of this contemplation, I "heard" an inner command arising from the depths of my soul. The initial words of this inner guidance were, "First, you have to share what you've learned."

Along with this directive came a bird's eye view of all the varied experiences I'd had throughout my life, along with a glimpse of my deeper soul goals. Within this vision, all my different life scenarios and phases – from youth, to college, to a monastic life, to Hollywood, to this time of aloneness and infirmity – seemed to all fit together and make perfect sense.

That moment of seeing it all fit together and make sense was truly a great gift, which uplifted me into a whole new level of spiritual happiness. Right in the midst of those challenging times came this most precious gift – an ability to see my life from above and beyond my personal, individual self. With this vision, I entered a new level of trust in the perfect orchestration of life.

I'd also been given a clear directive from within. I now had a new guiding light for arranging my priorities into the next phase. I was to share what I learned, whenever and however I was guided to do it in each moment. I knew that if I could approach this undertaking with the right attitude and pure motivation, God, the universal Good, would also support and work together with me, protecting, empowering, and guiding my steps. I didn't feel a sense of burden in fulfilling this command to "share what you've learned." Instead, I experienced a sense of willingness, faith, and surrender – and with that, came a great flow of spiritual happiness.

While focusing on my deeper priorities to love, serve, and trust God, I also found that the right people, projects and experiences started to naturally arrive in my life at just the right time – including *this* book, which came about during lunch at a café next to the sacred gardens and hermitage in Encinitas, California, where the Indian sage, Paramahamsa Yogananda, wrote the spiritual classic "Autobiography of a Yogi" many decades ago.

On this day, I had been running some errands, and decided to stop and have lunch at a small outdoor restaurant, called "Swami's Café," which I hadn't been to in years. While enjoying my meal, I overheard a fellow at the table next to me asking the waitress about Yogananda and the gardens across the street. She responded that she didn't really know much about them.

Being the helpful type, I kindly piped in to tell the man what he wanted to know, and we ended up having a friendly and interesting discussion. It turns out that this fellow was Avery Cardoza, one of the publishers for Cold Spring Press, who was visiting San Diego for two days, and had somehow ended up at Swami's Café. Soon, I was writing "Secrets of Spiritual Happiness" for their new "Secrets of…" series, and here we are.

This is one example of how arranging and rearranging our priorities can help to bring us into "the flow." When our priorities are clear, the universe is better able to work with us in bringing them into form. We're not just walking recklessly through life, tossing out conflicting desires and resolutions with every step. Clearer priorities tend to bring clearer results.

When we enter that deep spiritual flow, the universe itself supports and guides our steps. For example, our inner intuition may give a *thumb's up* or a *thumb's down* regarding what we are doing in each moment. By listening to this inner guidance and approaching our lives with strength, wisdom, and surrender, we can assess what is right for us, and what is best left for someone else to do.

Consider how much time you spend on arranging your furniture, your office, your kitchen, garage, finances, and household work. Arranging your priorities deserves even more care and effort than these other tasks!

Taking time to arrange your priorities is truly a great step towards attaining spiritual happiness.

❧

Don't Let Others Tell You What Will Make You Happy

Once, an old man, a boy, and a donkey were traveling from one town to another. They decided that the boy would ride the donkey, and the old man would walk alongside. While moving down the road, they passed a group of townsfolk, who began speaking among themselves, saying what a shame it was for such a strong, young boy to be riding on the donkey, leaving this old, frail man to walk alongside. The boy overheard their words, and, feeling ashamed, suggested that the old man should ride the donkey, and that he would walk alongside.

A while later, they passed another group of people, who began commenting on how shocking it was to see this man riding the donkey, while making such a small boy walk. The two overheard their comments, and decided that they should both just walk and put an end to all these opinions.

Eventually, they passed some more villagers, who began to laugh at how silly it was for these two to be walking when they had a perfectly good donkey to ride. The man and the boy decided that maybe the critics were right, and they decided to both ride the donkey.

Soon, they ran into another group of people who were aghast to see such animal cruelty. What a load to put on this poor little creature! Hearing their words, the man and boy felt terrible. They wanted to give the poor donkey a break, and decided to carry the donkey for the rest of their way.

While crossing a bridge, they lost their grip on the animal, and he fell into the river, to be seen no more. The moral of this story: If you try to please everyone, you will eventually lose your ass!

> *The majority is never right. Never, I tell you! That's one of these lies in society that no free and intelligent man can help rebelling against. Who are the people that make up the biggest proportion of the population, the intelligent ones or the fools? I think we can agree it's the fools, no matter where you go in this world, it's the fools that form the overwhelming majority.*
> **– Henrik Ibsen**

Many people spend their whole lives pursuing what other people have concluded happiness is, or what the media has told them that happiness is, or what companies that sell things have advertised happiness to be. Our mission is to break those lies and to find our true happiness. Then, we won't end up working hard all our lives to accomplish things that never bring true happiness.

How can you be truly happy if you're always squelching your inner wisdom, guidance, and dreams just to fit into other people's concepts and expectations, or to fit into worldviews that don't do justice to the depths of your deep soul intelligence and aspirations?

What if your deepest soul calling is to become a priest, and you are born into a community of staunch atheists? What if you love to study philosophy, but find that your friends and family are not interested in anything but the outermost appearances of things? What if your deepest aspiration is to help people, but your partner vehemently encourages you to accept a job that takes advantage of others, but pays well?

All seekers of spiritual happiness must find a balance between their true goals and beliefs and the expectations of those around them.

One reason I enjoyed living in the monastic ashram during the 1980's is because it was a treasure house of diverse and interesting views. This was a place where I could also explore and expand my own beliefs, ideas, and worldview. All kinds of folks found their way to meet and spend time with the two great spiritual teachers who have been the hubs of this spiritual path from the 1960's until present day. We had everyone from spiritual eccentrics, to CEO's, to barefoot hippie types, to the most famous celebrities of the day. I lived with everyone from tarot card readers, to French aristocrats, to accomplished scientists, to beautiful models, to all kinds of pre-"new-age" spiritual characters – since my ashram stay took place before spirituality became so mainstream.

I remember relishing the idea that so many different kinds of people could live together and still maintain their own uniqueness, while collectively striving to grow spiritually. For the most part, we would respect one another's individuality. After all, we were on a spiritual path that exhorted us to honor our individual connection to the creative power of God, and also to greet one another with great respect and love, and with all our hearts.

Nevertheless, even in this eclectic environment, we'd still encounter those who enjoyed judging others and trying to make everyone fit into their little boxes of "appropriate behavior," and "proper thought." In fact, you'll hardly find this quality entrenched anywhere as much as in spiritual communities!

Therefore, the same courageous independence that would allow us to actually seek and spend time with a guru was also necessary to help us strengthen and maintain our inner truth within the sphere of the spiritual community. We'd have to learn to hold our own and to develop great inner strength so we could stay focused on our personal wisdom, knowledge, and aspirations, and walk our own path, even within the larger path.

Each of us spends time in various circles of communities – from families, to schools, to religious organizations, to work situations. In each of these groupthink scenarios, it is our duty to learn from others without selling out what we know is right. If, for example, we can see that the emperor has no clothes – as in the children's tale – we may not run around blabbing about it to everyone, unless we enjoy being an activist; however we can at least contemplate and acknowledge within ourselves that the emperor is, indeed, quite naked.

Staying true to what we know may sometimes require that we not be too concerned with what others may think or say about us. It requires a certain self-contained confidence and faith – a freedom from marriage to the norm. Some may think that you're eccentric if you follow your dreams. That's okay. Just be eccentric enough to feel happy about their view of your being eccentric. Feel grateful to yourself for being honest, creative, and original in your approach to life.

Of course, this advice is coming from someone who is occasionally considered to be somewhat eccentric. Recently, while telling a friend about some neuroscientists I've been working with, I mentioned that we have gotten along very well, although I might be a little eccentric for them. My friend said, "You're a little eccentric for everybody! You're the eccentric's eccentric!"

Some might interpret a comment like this as negative, but I felt very happy while hearing my friend's words – yes, compared to many, I am eccentric. And in exchange for being considered as an eccentric by some, I get to be myself and speak my truth, at least to a greater degree than I would if my goal were to please everyone's judgments and expectations of what "proper people" should look like. I get to wear comfortable clothes and think comfortable thoughts. I get to keep my focus on God's presence any time I'd please – especially now, having written several spiritual books. In fact, being spiritual and happy is now my job!

Through God's grace and self-effort, I've been able to create a life that is in greater harmony with my nature, and in which I feel more comfortable expressing my true thoughts and inspirations to fulfill the inner command I've received, to "share what you've learned."

> *The individual has always had to struggle to keep from being overwhelmed by the tribe. If you try it, you will be lonely often, and sometimes frightened. But no price is too high to pay for the privilege of owning yourself.*
> – **Friedrich Nietzsche**

It's always a balance. Part of the challenge is to find out how much we want to fit into the majority views of society and how much to stay true to our deepest, unique, and perhaps even eccentric self.

The key to having spiritual happiness along with outer happiness is to find a balance where you can be true to yourself, while still fitting into society in a positive way. You *could* choose to just pursue your inner dreams without any consideration for society's opinions, but that might end up leading to an experience of spiritual happiness without outer happiness. It's up to each one of us to find the right balance of outer acceptance and spiritual happiness for our personal natures, lessons, and goals.

Now, I'd like to share with you one of my ongoing lessons in encountering others who have wanted to tell me what would make me happy. I've had a series of experiences regarding my choice of clothing style that have given me numerous opportunities to explore this balance between being congenial to those around me, while still being true to my personal nature and style. The basic fact is that I don't like wearing any clothes or shoes that are uncomfortable. My natural tendency is to dress simply, naturally, and for maximum comfort.

Through the years, every now and then, someone who knows me will come up with a brilliant brainstorm. "If only she dressed better, she'd be so much more attractive!" I've experienced this scenario many times, and with various friends. They get that bright look in their eyes, as though nobody has ever thought of this epiphany before. As they'd gently broach their offer to help me "put together a few outfits," I'd be thinking, "Here we go again!"

At one point, while living a monastic life at the ashram, I was given a substantial clothing allowance. One of the more fashionable women who lived there – a manager's wife, no less – offered to go shopping with me so she could help me choose more fashionable clothes. This woman also had that glint of "makeover time!" in her eyes. I was trying to be surrendered to giving new clothing suggestions a try, and ended up with several bags full of things like tight jeans and itchy wool sweaters. I gave them a chance, but in fact, they didn't have a chance of becoming a part of my comfortable wardrobe. "Let's see, what shall I wear today – the stiff, tight jeans with the clingy, itchy blouse, or these nice khaki pants and soft flannel shirt? Hmmm…" This reminds me of the story about a dog with a curly tail.

Once there was a dog that had a very curly tail. His owner wanted the dog to have a straight tail, and created a pipe to put over the tail. He'd pull the tail straight and placed the pipe over the straight tail. The tail would become straight. Then the owner took off the pipe, and zing! The tail would curl right back up. The owner would leave the pipe on the dog's tail for a day, a week, and then a month, but whenever he took the pipe off, the tail would curl right back up again.

This is how I was with all these friends who tried to get me to dress well. I tried to be open to upgrading my style, but found that the expectations of being "well-dressed" were uncomfortable in more ways than just the itchy, tight, fancy clothes that were being suggested. These styles weren't reflective of my nature, and trying to wear them created a sense of conflict and distance between my inner being and my outer presentation. I'm sure this is not unfamiliar to many who have to wear neckties or high-heeled shoes for their jobs (hopefully not at the same time!)

Learning to stay true to myself in this one area of clothing style also helped me learn to stay true to myself in other arenas. At the same time, I do try to be harmonious with the environment around me, whenever comfortably and honestly possible. It's always a balance.

Contemplate how you can maintain the integrity of your true beliefs in the midst of worldly expectations – to what degree and in what way. Some historical spiritual figures boldly espoused their spiritual wisdom and truth, and were martyred or crucified for their honesty. We are so fortunate today to have much of the world living in freedom. Therefore, let's take advantage of this blessed time, and take a chance on our dreams, whatever they may be. Trust in the truth that's inside of you.

08

Be Careful About the Company You Keep

Surround yourself with happy faces — people who are interested in growing and enjoying.
—Wayne Dyer

You are a temple of God walking through and upon this earth. You have a choice whether to let that temple get covered with dust, garbage, debris, and weeds, or whether you keep it shining with beautiful, bright, crystal clarity. Some combination seems to be the lot for most of us, and perhaps that's how it is meant to be, after all.

According to ancient spiritual sages who saw beyond the veils of this world, we are purity itself, existing in an environment of mixed purity and impurity. We are bright and beautiful lotus flowers blossoming forth through and above the muddy waters of worldly life. And, in fact, those muddy waters are also supplying some of the minerals and nutrients that feed the plant's health and beauty. In the same way, spiritual happiness is not about ignoring the world, but about paying attention to what is nurturing or harming your spirit, while rising above it all to shine your glory and beauty into the world.

The company we keep has a powerful effect on our ability to blossom fully. It's amazing how quickly good company can help bring us out of an agitated state of mind, and how quickly bad company can put us in one.

Of course, one goal on the journey of spiritual happiness is to become independent of outer circumstances. However, until we reach that great state of completely independent spiritual happiness, it makes sense to take care regarding the company we keep.

This is certainly an important secret of spiritual happiness: to be aware and careful about the company we are keeping – inside, outside, in relationships, and in books, movies and television programs. When-ever possible, choose to be around people, places, thoughts, and things that create greater spiritual happiness in your mind, heart and soul.

If you would like to create more peace and happiness in your life, you may also want to consider reducing the amount of time you spend with certain kinds of "media company" that agitate you, or that bring up images of violence or terror-filled scenes that you would never wish to create in your life.

In some cases, a dramatic situation or movie may give you some benefits, such as being a fairly harmless stress release or adrenaline boost, while in other cases, it will only create agitation, nightmares, and digestive troubles. It's up to you to be careful about the company you keep, whether in media or in people; and it's also up to you to decide what balance is right for you.

Some people are actually like walking horror films, always talking about the many tragedies and horrific stories that have fallen upon their lives and the lives of their friends. Our words also have great power, and so their relishing of every traumatic detail over and over may, in fact, be contributing to the conflagration of dreadfulness that they love to describe.

Personally, I try not to spend too much time with such folks, in part because their words are not positive and happiness-conducive. Also, I figure that if you meet someone and all their close friends have terrible and ongoing horror stories, then you just may consider whether you really want to add your name to their list of close friends!

Being careful about the company you keep is similar to being careful of the foods you eat. If you really pay attention to the effects of different foods on your body, then you'll have more control over your physical happiness. For example, you may eat a big greasy meal, and notice that you don't feel so good afterward. This gives you a chance to control how you're going to feel in the future, by choosing whether you really want to have another big greasy meal.

In the same way, pay attention to how you feel when you hang around certain "greasy" people, or go to certain types of places. Perhaps you can't always control the company you are in, such as in work or travel situations, nevertheless, you can still find ways to add more positive and inspiring company when you *do* have possession of the "remote control" of your life, such as during your off-work hours.

How do you feel when you take a brisk walk in the morning and watch the sunrise? How do you feel in the midst of whatever religious or spiritual gatherings you have chosen to participate in? How do you feel when you're with family, with friends, or in the company of those with whom you work? How do you feel when you watch violence on television or in a movie theatre? Maybe good, and maybe not so good. Be aware of how the vibrations of your body, mind, and soul feel as you move through your day in the company of various people, locations, and events. Then you'll have greater power to choose how you feel, and to hopefully choose happiness.

If you watch the news all evening, and find that you can't sleep because you're worried that terrorists are going to blow something up, or that the snipers might attack you, or that a serial killer might break into your house, then you may have created inner unhappiness by keeping the company of too much outer bad news.

For ten years of monastic life, I rarely watched the news, although I did work in the ashram's video department, and had access to a television for most of that time. However, with such a strong and intent focus on the eternal presence and on timeless spiritual teachings, I just didn't feel motivated to watch television very often at all. Pretty much the only things that I saw on television during the 1980's were Princess Diana's wedding to Prince Charles, a dramatic news announcement that the U.S. had just bombed Libya, and Michael Jackson singing and dancing to "Billie Jean," when he first unveiled the moonwalk dance step on Motown's twenty-fifth anniversary special.

Soon after leaving the ashram in 1989, I was hired to work on a news show in Los Angeles, where I was an editor and producer for several years. We actually managed to fill five hours of news every day – which was unheard of in those pre-cable news days. Yet, in spite of this abundance of news, I realized that I hadn't really missed all that much by skipping an entire decade of news. I caught up with the rest of society fairly quickly, although intriguing gaps did show up for a while – such as not knowing who certain celebrities were, and being unaware about various prominent events that had taken place in the world during my monastic decade.

While working on this news show, I had an opportunity to work with a phenomenally creative staff of reporters, writers, camera crew and post-production staff. I also saw that news shows are a business and a service, but a business first. The underlying goal is to increase viewer ratings without going over the line of ethics enough to get you written up negatively in the local paper – as one of the other stations in our town often did. All the news programs would run what were called "teases" to entice people to stay tuned and watch a story later in the day or later in the broadcast. Maybe some food was being recalled, or some other scary warning was being given, with that very serious newscaster face: "Your children may be in danger; details at eleven!"

News folks can tend to become somewhat numbed toward the daily string of disasters that they see, write, produce, and edit, all day, every day. The words that make up most news stories are words like murder, death, fire, disaster, showdown, fierce fighting — you get the picture. You can probably hear some of them right now just by scanning a few news stations, especially the ones that deal with the goings on of urban communities. As they used to say, "If it bleeds, it leads."

We news folks would tend to become desensitized to some of the emotional impact of such stories, because they were such an integral part of our daily jobs. About the only time we'd escape a daily flow of murders, fires, burglaries, and disputes was when there was a bigger, national story taking precedence, such as on election nights, or when we were working on special feature pieces about various interesting and hot topics.

Since I left that field, news shows have blended even more with the tabloid mentality, so that now a serial murder doesn't even have to be recent to be retold again and again through one of many "serial killers!" type series. With these somewhat numbed-out producers, writers, and anchors trying to grab the viewer with intense and enticing stories, teases, and intros, the viewing public eventually also becomes more numb to this massive flood of negative images and words being paraded on their television screens, every day and every night.

> *If we are forced, at every hour, to watch or listen to horrible events, this constant stream of ghastly impressions will deprive even the most delicate among us of all respect for humanity.*
> — **Cicero**

It is nearly impossible to escape this media blitz of destruction, sorrow, grief, loss, devastation, frustration, and sadness – with only occasional stories about the many who are doing something good. Avoiding negative stories and images in today's world would be nearly as miraculous as parting the Red Sea. It's as though everybody now lives a traumatic childhood, witnessing an ongoing series of horrors, cruelties, and heart-wrenching scenes from an early age. You can't really exist in today's world without knowing all the pain, sorrow, and trauma that exists all over the world.

As with everything else in life, much of the benefit or harm from the media comes from how we choose to use it. For example, becoming aware of troubles and pains across the globe can be a blessing if that inspires us to heal those problems.

Personally, I consider it a blessing to have life lessons ready to view on television any time I might want some material to enjoy or consider. With television, I can enjoy my peaceful and somewhat hermit lifestyle while still being able to keep up with the world, the news, and current trends. It also gives me an abundance of material for contemplation or writing, with the flick of a channel. As the humorist, Swami Beyondananda, likes to say, the purpose of this material world is to give us good material!

Remember, this media explosion is still a fairly new development on the human evolution scene. Television wasn't even close to being around at the turn of the twentieth century. Why, I'm not all that old, and TV's were rare and only black and white when I was very young. The last few generations are the only ones that grew up having scripted friends and extended families on television.

Only in recent decades have the network and cable stations turned to so much negative fare, although recent years have also shown some promising possibilities for using television and film to actually uplift people and our society – what a concept, using the media for good!

The proliferation of media can also bring other benefits, including entertainment, emotional release, humor, education about many cultures, and – especially with the move toward reality TV – countless lessons about the human experience, from the honorable to the pathetic. Quiz shows, talent and survival competitions, personal exposés, court battles, dating shows, and other kinds of reality television not only catch our voyeuristic attention, but also offer living models we can watch and study to learn more about how human beings act and react in different situations. With these observations, we can learn more about human nature, and can also begin to look more closely at understanding and improving our own personal natures.

Nevertheless, if you find yourself feeling unhappy while watching too much of certain kinds of shows, then by all means, do make use of that remote to change the station, or to turn the television off and do something more constructive with your time. Meditate! Contemplate! Write the book you've always wanted to write! Learn to cook a new dish. Help your children with their homework. Sing a song. Have a friendly conversation. Take a class. Go for a walk. Go to the gym. You know your life and your preferences — find some good inner or outer company that will uplift and inspire you with greater happiness.

Do your best to be around people who are good company – who want to be happy, and who want to see you be happy. And, most importantly, be good company for yourself, because that is the company you have for life.

☙

Don't Let Others Bring You Down

My faith demands that I do whatever I can, wherever I can, whenever I can, for as long as I can with whatever I have to try to make a difference.
– Jimmy Carter

Once, the sage Tulsidas saw a scorpion that was struggling to escape from a river. The scorpion was about to drown, when Tulsidas reached over and saved it. The scorpion immediately stung Tulsidas. In shock, Tulsidas dropped the scorpion back into the waters, where it began struggling again to keep from drowning. Tulsidas again reached over and picked up the scorpion to save it from drowning. The scorpion stung Tulsidas once again. This happened three more times, before Tulsidas was finally able to toss the scorpion to safety in the wooded land around the river.

A man who had been watching this whole incident walked over to Tulsidas, and asked him, "Are you crazy?"

Tulsidas replied, "It is the scorpion's nature to sting, and it is my nature to be helpful to all beings. If the scorpion keeps its nature even in the face of death, why should I give up my compassionate nature in the face of his sting?"

One of the great challenges in life is to stay true to the best of what exists inside of us. Others can either help to raise us up into greater levels of awareness, or they can keep us limited to their small views of who and what they think we are or should be. This is one reason why I enjoy spending time alone. In quiet and peaceful solitude, I find it much easier to remember my deeper wisdom, aspirations, and priorities, without getting as easily swept away by the desires and concepts of others.

At the same time, not everyone has such a loner's nature. Therefore, the key is to find friends and acquaintances who support your growth into being the best that you can be.

If you don't feel you have a choice about being in the company of folks who have distorted judgments about you, then you may want to use that experience as an opportunity to practice keeping your strength of character, even in the midst of their "scorpion stings."

When we stop being so concerned about what other people think of us, this one shift eliminates so many potential causes of unhappiness. All of a sudden, we're not worried about every pound we gain. We're not worried about being embarrassed from making a mistake, or about whether the clothes we're wearing have gone out of style, or about whether the people who we like to spend time with make us look good in other's eyes. With freedom from the judgments of others, we don't have to feel compelled to go under the knife so that others will approve of our breast size, or to worry if some of our active hair follicles start thinning, or if a few gray hairs or wrinkles start popping up here and there – which they most certainly will, if we live long enough to grow old.

> *The man who makes everything that leads to happiness*
> *depends upon himself, and not upon other men, has*
> *adopted the very best plan for living happily.*
> – **Plato**

Instead of focusing on what others think about us, we can focus on what *we* think of ourselves. An entire arena of potential unhappiness is dissolved when we simply stop worrying so much about what others think of us.

With this one shift, you'll have the freedom to try something and then change your mind if you don't like it. You won't be worried that people will judge you for quitting, even when your goal in quitting one path is to pursue what you hope will be a better road. You can try and fail, and get right back up to try again if that is what your inner guidance says to do – without worrying that others will be gossiping about your initial failure. What do people know of your deepest aspirations and dreams, of your faith and hopes and unrealized potential? People usually only know what they can see, if that.

If we try to please people's judgmental perceptions and opinions all the time, we'll be spending a great deal of our focus, energy, and other resources on a superficial dance of outer appearances that ultimately dissolves. So many of the things we do that keep us from being happy, and so many of the things we don't do that would make us happy, come from concern over what other people might say or think about us.

Many have disregarded their deepest goals because they didn't want to disrupt whatever plans their family had made on their behalf. Some may have been scheduled to go to college, but found something else that was their true calling. Yet, many would squelch that inner passion and longing, just so nobody will get mad at them for going against expectations. Entire lives have been built on trying to please and impress others, with entire dreams for true happiness left, lost and abandoned, by the roadside.

What's important in living a happy life is to have what *you* need and want, and not what other people will be impressed by, or what they think you should need or want. And your other job is to strive to keep your needs and wants in harmony with your higher nature, and with the deep inner wellspring of soul wisdom that knows exactly what you truly need in every moment. Of course, it is fine and well to listen and take into account the advice of those whose opinions you respect, yet, once you are officially an adult in society's eyes, your life is your responsibility. Don't let others bring you down!

Maybe you were born with a talent and love for playing musical instruments, but your macho father pushed you to spend your after school time in sports. Maybe you had spiritual or artistic aspirations that were squelched by those who wanted you to focus on endeavors they thought were more important. Maybe your parents wanted to be grandparents, and you decided to have children to fulfill those expectations.

I remember years ago, while I was living in the monastery, my grandmother tried to convince me to marry and have children. Her main reason that one should have kids was so you'll have someone to take care of you when you're old. What a gamble that is: spend two decades of your life slaving away for a child you may not even want, with expectations of great rewards in the distant future – and hope that you don't end up with a Goth freak who hates you and runs away from home, or one of any other variety of possible outcomes that might keep you from getting your expected returns from this substantial investment. So many unwanted situations come from this one quality of caring too much about what other people think of us.

Even if you spend all your efforts to please everybody, truthfully, in the end, none of that really matters so much. You may do everything that people want you to do, and then do one thing wrong, and find yourself being harshly judged anyway.

I first learned not to let others bring me down as a child, when my family moved from a simple, poorer city into a much wealthier suburb. My sister and I experienced a great deal of prejudice from the other children, most of whom were much more well-dressed and well cared for than we were. Of course, children can sometimes reveal the more animalistic tendencies of the untamed human nature, and I experienced many encounters with young ones who thought they could bring themselves up by pushing others down. Although this was not a pleasant experience, it did teach me to hold my own in life, and to not let others bring me down – try, though they might.

For several years, until finally moving into the more pleasant and friendly waters of junior high school, I experienced being somewhat of an outcast. Although the experience was often challenging, during this time, I also gained some precious blessings. Unlike many of my fellow classmates, I was not so focused on social hierarchies or childish spats. I learned to enjoy being alone. I became more inwardly focused, and found a certain peaceful enjoyment there. I learned to watch the world, and to listen to my inner soul, even though I didn't call it that at the time.

This inner growth prepared me, by age twenty, to make the biggest leap of trust that I'd made up till that point. After being brought up as an atheist my whole life, I left right in the middle of college to pursue a monastic life. I moved into the ashram of my guru, Swami Muktananda.

For me, leaving college to move into an Indian ashram at age twenty was definitely an unexpected twist – not only for me, but for my friends and family as well. After all, this took place in 1980, long before topics such as spirituality, yoga, gurus, or meditation became familiar and prevalent in society. About the only spiritual books you could find in those days were pop-psychology paperbacks and old, occult-style books. Moving into an ashram was simply not an acceptable choice to make in our suburban town.

Yet, I thank God that I found the strength to follow my heart's calling, in spite of having to take the heat of other people's burned expectations. In fact, because of the independent spirit I'd developed during my childhood years, I really didn't feel very much heat at all. I was inwardly guided to take this surprising step, and nobody was going to be able to keep me down.

The next ten years of monastic life transformed and uplifted me from the inside, out. I thank God every day that I was able to follow my own guidance instead of relying on the group mentality of my society at that time. From this successful leap of faith, I learned that you don't need to have the approval of everyone else in order to be happy. Therefore, my suggestion is to keep your focus on what you believe is right, while remaining open to any helpful suggestions that come from those around you.

Even to progress in our spiritual evolution, we have to have some detachment from the opinions and expectations of others. For example, if you have evolved to a point of seeing beyond certain limited perspectives, well, you can be sure that people who still have those limited perspectives aren't going to want you to come around and mess with them. I remember years ago when, if I mentioned to someone that I did yoga, they would look shocked at my doing something so weird, or they may have made fun of me for doing something so strange. Of course, now yoga is all over the place, but if I had waited to enjoy its benefits until the rest of society caught up to it, then I would have missed the best opportunities of my life.

Although you may find it beneficial to fit into whatever culture and social system you've taken birth into, you don't have to be limited by such structures in your own mind, heart, and soul. Don't let others bring you down.

For example, if you believe that death is not bad, but is rather the passing of a soul into heaven, or back into its original nature, then don't let the anguish and sorrow of others keep you from trusting your higher vision when someone you know passes over. This is where the dual awareness explained earlier can also come in handy. You can use the idea of dual awareness to feel and express the appropriate sadness for having lost someone, while also remaining anchored in faith and trust that all is well, and that the person is cradled in God's Loving Hands.

Don't let others keep you from singing the song you are here to sing in this grand symphony of life. Find your song. Find your essence. Find your dreams. Find your greatest destiny. Find your path of harmony, and you'll also find spiritual happiness.

ભ

Don't Bring Others Down!

We are all full of weakness and errors, let us mutually pardon each other our follies – it is the first law of nature.
—**Voltaire**

Just as you don't want to spend too much time worrying about what others think of you, you also don't want to spend too much of your time thinking about what others should do – judging how someone else looks, what they own, how they behave, or what hidden motivations they may have.

Modern society has gotten into some bad habits lately. One of the more harmful habits is when people, individually, and especially as a group, tear down those who are most precious to ourselves and to humanity as a whole. Many great leaders — political, religious, and otherwise — have a mountain of positive characteristics, yet we look for some spot of taint in them. Modern society has done this with everyone from presidents, to stock market savvy domestic goddesses, to kings of pop, divas of R&B, and even Mother Teresa, for goodness sake!

We sometimes look for taint in people, instead of just enjoying their offerings of talent, beauty, love, and skills. Network and cable news shows have also succumbed to this habit of tabloid mentality –

bringing its tendrils into nearly every home where television is watched. Gossip has gone mainstream.

Of course, it is human nature to be curious and to want to know personal details about others. That, in itself, isn't such a bad trait. Interest is one thing; destructive gossip is another. Some journalists seem to relish magnifying each stain into some murky mixture of true and untrue headline gossip. Raucous and pretentious news show debates create national obsessions about every morbid, shocking, enticing, and risqué detail in the life of whatever public figure is being tossed to the gossip lions today. As a result of the media's propagation of this bad habit, we've become a gossip mongering society. This is a problem, because gossip destroys not only the object of gossip, but also those who are doing the gossiping, and the fabric of society as well.

Nevertheless, blessings can be found anywhere, and one blessing that has come from this bad habit of journalistic gossiping is that we've finally learned, once and for all, that nobody is perfect, except in the universal sense of spiritual perfection. If you're here in form, you have lessons to learn.

This understanding makes it easier for us to also acknowledge our own frailties, without getting into a swamp of judgmental internal gossip about ourselves. Having witnessed the media's array of spicy personal revelations about just about every well-known person in history, we can come to the mature realization that nobody is absolutely perfect in every way, and through the eyes of every judge.

If we expect perfection from those who have achieved some greatness or shown a willingness to serve society, then we box these people into a life that fits into our expectations. They may feel obliged to put on a face that doesn't reflect *their* inner beliefs. Eventually, that distorted outer face may foster an inner environment that brings about distorted actions that go against their own religious, political, or essential beliefs – giving even more fodder for more gossiping.

Instead of coming into their own deeply guided relationship with God or their own deep wisdom, some spiritual, artistic, and political leaders may have to spend much of their time and efforts worrying about how their actions will be perceived by the "viewing public," or the "voting public," or by those tabloid journalists who are licking their chops in hopes of finding the next explosive or salacious rumor to reveal publicly. This is how society unintentionally brings down its greatest achievers, with these gems of humanity being crucified again and again by the errant soldiers of judgment, animosity, jealousy, and greed.

Therefore, let's create greater happiness all the way around by practicing acceptance, tolerance, and respect toward ourselves as well as toward others.

One way to respect others is to stop participating in the group mentality of criticism and gossip. Both publicly and in our own lives, we can stop looking so hard at others to find and drag out any actions or qualities that appear to be faults to our own faulty eyes. We can also look upon those who have stumbled with a sense of compassion, and an acknowledgement that "there, but for the grace of God, go I."

> *Why do you see the speck in your brother's eye, but do not notice the log in your own eye? Or how can you say to your brother, "Friend, let me take out the speck in your eye," when you yourself do not see the log in your own eye? You hypocrite! First take the log out of your own eye, and then you will see clearly to take the speck out of your brother's eye.*
> — Jesus Christ

Why not love, respect, and support our leaders instead of tearing them down? Why not love and respect ourselves as well? Why not focus on people's good qualities? Why not be grateful and appreciative for those who have offered themselves to various avenues of world service?

Why turn every famous and accomplished person into pabulum for the tabloid gossip industry?

This doesn't mean that we have to hide anyone's frailties or pretend that they have no faults, but we also don't have to distort and exaggerate their mistakes into big blockbuster headlines. How would you like it if people looked for slip-ups to report in every move *you* make?

Respect for one another is one of the foundations of spirituality – do unto others as you would have them do unto you. If we can learn to truly welcome one another with love and respect, spiritual happiness will shine brightly in our lives and in the world.

03

Think Well of Everyone

All that we are is the result of what we have thought; it is founded upon our thoughts, it is made up of our thoughts. If a man speaks or acts with an evil thought, pain follows him, as the wheel follows the foot of the ox that draws the carriage. If a man speaks or acts with a pure thought, happiness follows him, like a shadow that never leaves him.
—**Gautama Buddha**

One secret of spiritual happiness is to stay a bit naïve in terms of suspicions about others. Unless there is some possibility of actual damage or danger that may arise from their actions, it may be best to just assume as much as you can that people are coming from a good place. The key, once again, is balance – to think as well as possible about others, while still being vigilant and realistic, depending on the particular circumstances.

When I find myself in the company of those who bring up not-so-positive thoughts in my mind – such as people who behave rudely, or who act petty or unkind – I'll usually turn my attention within, toward the inner wisdom, and contemplate if this experience may be God's way of letting me know that this is possibly a place where I shouldn't spend more time than necessary.

Certainly, God is well versed in the fine arts of behavior modification – a psychological term for using reward and punishment to guide and train a person or animal. Instead of just wallowing in a swamp of negative thinking about others, I may consider whether those challenging experiences, thoughts, and feelings may actually be an inner guidance or universal suggestion to make a change in my outer life or inner attitudes.

One way to interpret the presence of troubling people in your life may be to ask whether you are meant to reduce your proximity and time with such people. Another interpretation would be to ask whether you might have been brought together with these challenging people to find greater strength inside yourself. Or, perhaps you are meant to help them in the face of their troubles. After all, we are often called upon to be the hands of angels for those around us. Sometimes we are also brought into the company of those who can help teach what we need to learn – whether through their good or bad examples. One key to spiritual happiness is to find an interpretation that allows us to focus on something positive whenever possible.

Ultimately, the basis of thinking well of everyone is to truly think well of ourselves. When we recognize and identify with our own greatness, negative thoughts and emotions, such as anger, hatred, and revenge, simply have no place to sit. Our "house" is so clean that there is no place for the bugs and mice of negative thinking. There is nothing for the cockroaches of judgment and criticism to eat. With faith and compassion, we seek to love and serve, rather than to criticize and judge.

In fact, thinking negatively about others actually affects you more than it affects them. For example, if you imagine an evil action, thought, or plot in someone else's mind – then whether there actually is an evil intent in that person's mind, there is most certainly now one in yours! Remember, if it's in your mind, it's in *your* mind!

Obviously, if we always try to assume the best about people, our naïve innocence may be disappointed and proved wrong at times. However, at least our minds will be creating positive images instead of negative ones. It is more conducive for spiritual happiness to think well of others and sometimes have that trust broken, than it is to distrust from the start. Think well of others, think well of yourself, and enjoy the gentle equanimity of spiritual happiness.

෫

Too Many Expectations
Lead to Disappointment

If you pick up a starving dog and make him prosperous,
he will not bite you; that is the principal difference
between a dog and a man.
– Mark Twain

The more that we expect from others, the more we are opening ourselves to being disappointed. Let me tell you a story about someone who had a big expectation, and a spiritual one, at that.

Some years ago a successful American businessman had a serious identity crisis, and deeply desired to know the meaning of life. He sought help from therapists and counselors, but nothing ever came of his efforts. Nobody could tell him what he wanted to know.

Eventually, the man learned of a venerable and incredibly wise guru who lived in a mysterious and most inaccessible region of the Himalayas. The businessman came to believe that this guru was the one person who could tell him what life meant, and what his role in it ought to be. With great faith and many expectations, the man sold all his worldly possessions. Eagerly, he began his search for this all-knowing guru.

The former businessman spent eight years wandering from village to village throughout the Himalayas in an effort to find this elusive master. Then, one blessed day, he chanced upon a shepherd who told him where the guru lived and how to reach the place.

It took the man nearly another year of intense austerity to find the hidden location, but he eventually did find his way to the mountaintop abode. There he came upon his guru, who was indeed venerable — in fact, well over one hundred years old. The guru consented to help him, especially when he learned of all the sacrifices the man had made to meet him.

With a compassionate smile, the guru asked, "My son, what can I do for you?"

"I must know the meaning of life," whispered the man, with eager anticipation.

The guru replied without hesitation. "Life," he said, "is a river without end." The guru settled back after answering the man's question.

"A river without end?" asked the man in startled surprise and emerging anger. "After coming all this way to find you, all you have to tell me is that life is a river without end?"

The guru was shaken and shocked. "You mean it's not!?!"

✠

Be a Joyful Giver

Doing good to others is not a duty. It is a joy, for it increases your own health and happiness.
—**Zoroaster**

Giving and receiving are like inhaling and exhaling your breath.

- However deeply you inhale and receive the air is also how deeply you are able to give and breathe out.

- However deeply you exhale and give what you have received, that is how deeply you will be able to inhale and receive.

- If you only want to receive and receive and hoard all that you've received, you'll suffocate.

- If you only want to give and give, without being open to receive, then you'll suffocate.

- Deep giving and deep receiving with all of your being will bring the most nourishment and health into your life and into the world.

You can tell how happy somebody is by how joyfully they give. When people are happy, they are naturally kind, patient, loving, and generous. Don't you find that it is much easier to be kind and patient when you're happy? If you're happy and someone takes a little extra time to go through the grocery line in front of you, it's no big deal. You're even able to allow someone to go ahead of you if they're in a hurry or have only a few items. Happy people are nice people. Happy people are effortless givers.

When you are happy, your gratitude wants to give something back, to lift someone else into happiness. Happiness is never petty or jealous. Happiness is loving and joyous. Happiness wishes to see good things happen to everyone.

If someone you know is not showing qualities of loving generosity, then – even if they seem to have more than you – your best call is to say a prayer on their behalf. Someone who cannot give cannot truly be happy. Even a multi-millionaire is but a pauper if he or she cannot give.

One of my favorite experiences of giving came while I was working at a Los Angeles news station that was owned by Disney.

Whenever there was a big disaster, the station executives would order in pizzas or sandwiches so that we could work without taking a full lunch break. Even now, when a disaster hits, I sometimes think of pizza.

One day, we were in the midst of one "breaking news" disaster or another, and the executive producers had ordered in sandwiches for the whole newsroom of about 60 or so people. They were always kind enough to order a vegetarian meal for me, and when my time came for a quick lunch, I sat down near the front door, picked up half of my sandwich, and began to eat.

In the meantime, the president and CEO of Disney, Michael Eisner, came in to visit our newsroom for the first time. I'd recently read several magazine articles about how Mr. Eisner had made tens of millions of dollars in stock options that year. He was standing right near me, chatting with the news director, when Mr. Eisner spotted the bag of sandwiches. I overheard him mentioning that he hadn't eaten all day, and that he was very hungry. Then, he asked if there were any vegetarian sandwiches available.

The news director glanced over at me chomping on my half-eaten sandwich – we both knew I had the only vegetarian meal in the place.

I thought, "When else am I going to have a multi-billionaire beg half a sandwich from me?" I wrapped up the uneaten half and offered it to Mr. Eisner with a friendly smile. "Here's half of a vegetarian sandwich for you!" He accepted and gratefully ate the gift.

> *What can one person do? There's something going on in your workplace, in your family, in your life, where Spirit is saying, "I've got you uniquely placed, because there's something I would do through you. For this I have created you. For this I have called you into being. You are free, to be and do all that God created you to be."*
> – Mary Manin Morrissey

One of the best ways to increase your own spiritual happiness is to help someone in the right way. This doesn't mean helping them while thinking that they owe you anything, or thinking proudly "I am saving this person, I'm helping this person." Rather, you can help others with a sense of humility and gratitude that God is helping them through you. This will sanctify your gift, and will also sanctify your experience of giving. When you learn to taste the sweetness of being a joyful giver, then you're most certainly also developing a taste for the gourmet delicacy of spiritual happiness.

Helping somebody creates a whole different kind of feeling in your being. If you're having a hard time in life and don't think you are feeling happy, help somebody. If you can find happiness in helping others, then you'll always be able to find some way to create happiness, in any circumstance. When you help someone, your heart warms, and spiritual happiness shows its smiling face to you.

Try it today. The next time you're driving and somebody wants to come into your lane, feel honored to have the opportunity to serve that person and to help him or her to safely and easefully merge into your lane. Know that divinity exists in every person, every driver, every waiter, every cashier, and every security guard.

See God in each other.
– **Baba Muktananda**

Always strive to give more than you receive — to people, to this world, and to God. Of course, outdoing God is ultimately impossible, since God is the giver of all — but the striving will make you happy!

☙

Be a Blessing

Some cause happiness wherever they go; others whenever they go.
—Oscar Wilde

Once upon a time, a king and his men were on their way to hunt, when they saw a simple fellow riding his donkey on the trail ahead of them. In that kingdom, seeing a donkey was considered to be a bad omen. The king was furious. He had been planning for this hunting trip all month, and now this man on the donkey had ruined the whole thing. "Go beat him!" the King commanded his men. They beat the man severely, and then the hunting party went on its way.

That day, the hunt went exceptionally well – in fact, it was the most successful hunt the king had ever had. On his way back to the palace, the king saw that same area of the road where they'd passed the man on his donkey. He felt a little guilty about having his men beat someone who had ended up being a very good omen.

The next morning, the king told his soldiers to bring the man to the castle, so he could apologize to him. The badly bruised man was brought to the king's courtyard.

SECRETS OF SPIRITUAL HAPPINESS

"I want to apologize to you," the king expressed, "It seems that you and your donkey were good omens, after all. Our hunt went exceptionally well."

"Well, your majesty," the man replied, "I saw *your* face yesterday morning, and look at my body – it's black and blue from head to toe. Tell me, O King, who is a good omen, and who is a bad omen?"

The finest road to spiritual happiness is to do your very best to be a blessing to everyone you see and to everyone you know. Even if you think someone has done something awful to you, you can still train yourself to wish well for him or her, although it may be a struggle at first. In fact, I always say that one way to receive my blessing is to get me angry, because instead of saying what my emotions might like to say — which might make this book R-rated, so I'll leave it to your imagination — when the person's name comes up, I'll often say "God bless him," or "God bless her." I've even come close to suggesting that some folks could just go "bless" themselves.

Getting into a habit of giving your blessings may start out feeling somewhat uncomfortable, strange, or insincere, because most of us are relatively unaware of our own, truly awesome power to give blessings. However, with gratitude and faith, giving blessings comes naturally. Once you see and appreciate all the blessings in your life, your gratitude for your own blessings will naturally inspire you to want to be a blessing to others, no matter who they are or what they have done or not done to or for you. If they are good, you'll want to bless them; and if they are bad, you'll want to bless them twice.

> *The highest exercise of charity is charity towards the uncharitable.*
> – J. S. Buckminster

Giving blessings is an especially important secret to spiritual happiness, because our wishes of blessings for others come back to us in many ways. You can think of this whole universe as being one big "I'm rubber, you're glue." If you offer abundant blessings and wishes of happiness for everyone, then that's likely what you'll find appearing in your own life as well.

You can even give blessings to people without telling them. In fact, this can be a more selfless form of blessing, because you're not doing it so the person will like you or give you something back when *you* are in need. In the silence of your heart, you can send unconditional blessings to a friend, or to the whole world – in a simple but heartfelt gift, offered beneath the blanket of physical reality, in the realm of spiritual happiness.

Right now, take a moment to offer a prayer and blessing for every being on this planet — pray for grace to manifest as whatever would be a blessing for them right now. And may God bless you too!

CB

Finding Grace in Challenges and Blessings From Tragedy

> *Every day God has a new challenge for the joy of one who loves Him. Such a lover of God never undermines these divine surprises. He knows that whatever God sends his way is meant to turn him into a perfect offering.*
> —Gurumayi Chidvilasananda

Our responsibility in life is what we give to the world in response to whatever experiences are given to us.

When difficulties come, see if you can look at them as challenges that are intended to refine, purify, or strengthen your soul. Some people also like to think of challenges as karma retributions for actions they've performed – that they did something wrong in their past, perhaps even in a so-called past lifetime, and that act has now boomeranged back from the cosmic scorekeeper as their present woes.

Personally, I prefer to keep my focus and interpretations on the idea of challenges as being lessons and gifts in an ultimately benevolent universe. This interpretation makes logical sense to me, and also allows me to grow without having to constantly descend into not-so-happy arenas such as guilt and self-condemnation.

I choose to think of God as a good and kind God, who is only tough when that's the only way we can learn certain lessons. This is an example of choosing a world-view and God-view that helps to create greater spiritual happiness in our mind, heart, and soul. Your world- and God-views are for you to discern and choose; I'm just sharing some thoughts about how I've come up with mine.

Although none of us really knows how this whole *human being in a big universe* thing works, we can still choose to contemplate worldviews that contribute to our comfort and happiness. If you live your life thinking that God loves you, and that thought helps you to be a happy person, to perform good actions, and to ride the waves of life with a steady faith and joy, well then, does it even matter if God really does love you or not? (Of course *He* does – I'm just making a point!)

With the right attitude, we may find that life's tragedies can actually bring wonderful blessings, because they have the potential to shake our worlds and create an opening for grace and growth to enter through doors that may have been previously crusted over by complacency, boredom, pride, desires, and expectations.

The United States of America went through a *group tragedy* just after the turn of this millennium, with the "9-11" terrorist attacks. The whole country came together to mourn, and, in fact, the entire world came together to mourn. For several weeks after terrorists ran those planes into the World Trade Center buildings, the Pentagon, and the field in Pennsylvania, our whole world was steeped in goodness and goodwill.

One website showed an amazing array of photos from just about every country, with beautiful memorials and mourning faces. Hearts across the world were united. How grand it was.

That precious time didn't last too long because many agendas were waiting in the arenas of politics and human aggression, but while we were in that short but sweet "golden sky after the storm" phase, we were glorious, globally. Humanity loved; humanity cared. Celebrities came together and humbly offered their skills to do what artists are supposed to do — using their God-given talents to inspire and create more goodness across the lands. A world full of prayers and blessings arose to counter the evil that had shown its face.

Certainly, this tragic event did not go to waste in terms of giving us all food for thought and contemplation. Each person had to contemplate so many questions regarding this event. When we first saw images of airplanes hitting those twin towers, every one of us went through a shift of some kind and some magnitude – a *soul quake*, if you will.

Such shocking moments can be the best times for practicing what the yogis call *sadhana*: our active participation in our spiritual and personal growth, through mental, physical, and spiritual efforts. When the heart is open and the mind is shocked, there is a rare opportunity to take great leaps in our spiritual awareness and consciousness. During such times, instead of just "freaking out," we can make extra efforts to keep our minds peaceful, and to contemplate deeper lessons behind the various outer events.

Usually in our lives, we can blow off this kind of inner spiritual contemplative work. Many people go through day after day of so-called living without even aspiring to see beyond simplistic, surface, black and white views of life. However, this 9-11 terrorist event really forced everybody to contemplate. You couldn't just blow this one off completely.

We watched executives leap to their death from the highest floors of those burning buildings. We saw faces filled with agony and shreds of precious hope parading through the streets of Manhattan, desperately showing photos of their missing loved ones. We heard story after story of tragedy, as well as of triumph. No movie could compare with what reality had brought forth. We realized and remembered how amazing life is — even, and perhaps especially in the midst of tragedy.

Powerful emotions gripped humanity. We had to contemplate topics such as death, hatred, intolerance, responsibility, and evil. We had to find more goodness within ourselves to balance out the horrors we were witnessing outside.

As the United States moved into a truly impressive state of prayer, I contemplated how it is often only in times of extreme personal tragedy – such as at the end of our lives – that we remember what is really important. The veil of worldly illusion falls away, and the soul lost remembers the soul eternal. Tragic events such as this can also give us opportunities to take great leaps of spiritual awareness and spiritual happiness right in the midst of our lives, if we are mature and lucid enough to make good use of those opportunities.

For months after this particular attack, television and movie studios also postponed showing negative images and violent movies. Instead, we watched images of some of the best that human nature has to offer — the dedication of workers at the site, the caring by so many anonymous helpers across the nation, stories of selfless sacrifice, the heartrending "singing cop," the generous giving of charity, inspired and moving interfaith memorial services, and patriotic offerings of time and skills by celebrities, as well as non-celebrities. Everybody had to bring forth some goodness inside of themselves to balance out the evil they'd witnessed. Americans had a rare opportunity to bless our motherland with song, and to show our gratitude and respect to a country that – thought clearly imperfect – has given many an opportunity to grow and learn our life lessons in an atmosphere of relative freedom. God bless America, and God bless the entire world.

An event as evil as these terrorist attacks actually has the potential to bring forth its opposite, goodness, because everything in the universe likes to stay in balance. So when you have something as evil and offensive as killing thousands of innocent people in a terrorist attack, each person who witnesses those events experiences some measure of good rising up within themselves. The heroism that many showed during and after this disaster is an example of how so much courage, love, and goodness can come forth in the midst of an explosion of evil and suffering.

This shows how even something as horrific as those attacks can end up bringing even more blessings than tragedy – depending on how we respond to it. The key is in what we do with the opportunity before it fades back into business as usual.

If we trust that this universe is in the hands of an omnipotent and omnipresent God, then we have to trust it even when things hit the fan. By practicing living with greater trust, we get better at it, just as with any other skill. We learn to live in the spiritual consciousness and the worldly consciousness simultaneously. And on the spiritual level, everything's fine, everything is destined, and everything is for our good, always.

When tough times hit the fan in your life, don't forget that every adverse event also carries the seed of potential growth to bring us individually and collectively into greater harmony. Learn to find grace in challenges and blessings from tragedy, and spiritual happiness will always be close at hand.

⊂∂

Always Deal with God

As mentioned in the beginning of this book, if the word "God" doesn't accurately represent your personal image and relationship, then please feel free to replace this word with any He, She, It, form, or formlessness that works for you. I'm using the term "God" in its general sense, and not as described by any one religion or tradition. The word "God" in this book refers to *generic God* – in plain white wrapping, and ready to be dyed and decorated by your own creative worldview.

> *God is a metaphor for that which transcends all levels*
> *of intellectual thought.*
> –Joseph Campbell

One great practice for spiritual happiness is to strive, in every situation, to deal primarily with God. For example when a potential employer is interviewing you for a job, or when you're hoping a landlord will rent you that apartment, instead of only asking or begging these folks in your mind, on paper, or in person to give you what you want, first ask God. Keep your attention focused on the divinity that expresses through every person and circumstance, and you will be uplifting every interaction into the arena of spiritual happiness.

Ask God for what you want, and ask God to guide you to want what is best. Trust God as the depths from whence all outer situations arise. Nothing ultimately comes from people or circumstances anyway; everything ultimately arises from the divinity – called by many names, including God – that creates and acts through all people and circumstances. Beneath, behind, and throughout all things is God, the dreamer of this dream of life. Therefore, you can always choose to address the God in anything and everything.

If you've got your eyes on God, then no matter what
people do, God will take care of you.
– Joyce Meyer

With a steady focus on God, you'll also be able to address your challenges with empowerment and faith. Instead of only trying to control outer events, you can also control your mind by asking, "What is God wanting to teach me? What can I learn from this challenge? How can I improve myself with this? What more can I give? How much more can I purify my emotions and uplift my motivations?"

When you are fortunate enough to be feeling love for someone or something, instead of only saying and thinking, "Oh, I love you, I love this house, I love this person, I love this cat, I love this job," you can add two words, "God as." I love God as this job, I love God as my dog, I love God as my friends, I love God in you, and I love God in me. This small step will bring greater happiness into your life, because you'll be giving your love to the source behind the external appearance, to the eternal truth beyond the facade of this ever-changing world.

By thanking and loving God in and as everything, you'll be wearing the right prescription glasses to see the depths of God's presence everywhere. External appearances come and go, but God *is*, *was*, and *will always be* right here and right now.

Thank God, give to God, love God, get mad at God, and make up with God. Consider that everything is the manifestation of a God who dearly loves you. Have the awareness that the universe loves you, and that God loves you. If some people are showing love to you, that's because God loves you so much that "He" is loving you through them. If nobody is loving you, then maybe God wants you all for "Himself." This way, you've got all the bases covered. Just start with an acceptance that God loves you completely, fully, and unconditionally, and deal with everyone and everything as a creation and expression of that loving God – who sometimes shows that love in strange ways!

With your eyes on the prize, the spiritual happiness in your heart will leap with joy as you bathe in the blessings of God's eternal presence and love.

❧

Let Go of "Punishment Mentality"

Behold, happy is the man whom God correcteth: therefore, despise not thou the chastening of the Almighty.
– Job 5:17

On our journey of spiritual happiness, there is a bit of cleaning up work for each of us to do. We've been given all kinds of blatant and subtle teachings throughout our lives—by our culture, by friends and families, in educational programs, and through the media. Some of these teachings may be true, some may be partially true, and some may not be true at all. Part of our job is to do a bit of weeding whenever possible, pulling out whatever weeds of wrong understanding may be keeping our beautiful blossoms from thriving.

One particularly questionable concept we need to look at is the fairly common image of a punishing God, who is waiting to shower wrath upon our lives, if we dare to displease "Him."

Perhaps such a concept is helpful in keeping those with animalistic desires from expressing harmful actions into the world. Without the threat of a punishing God, who knows what some people would do? But you're not like that, are you? You can be good just for the sake of your own inner satisfaction, and not because you're afraid of being punished from above, right?

God has lovingly created this exceptionally beautiful planet and given us all an opportunity to take birth here from the unknowable non-physical realm of the soul. Here, we live among the most exquisite and breathtakingly beautiful riches of nature, including a bountiful variety of colorful foods, with fresh, flowing waters, and all the glories of life that dance day and night upon this earth. I think it is obvious that *He* likes us.

Therefore, one good step toward spiritual happiness would be to stop thinking that God is waiting or wanting to punish us for our limitations and mistakes. Feelings of guilt and upset can actually cause us to create our own problems — like children who angrily break their own toys after being sent to their room for misbehaving.

This same archetypal pattern of punishment has also taken form in our society's ever-expanding prison system, which clearly demonstrates how ineffective this punishment mentality can be in the long run. It may take decades for society to find a better way to keep the masses in line than by using punishment mentality, however you can change your own personal approach right now. With the magical wand of your own mind, you can contemplate some of your inaccurate, world-given beliefs and begin to prune out those that create suffering in your life.

Small children are often punished by apparently magical parents, who somehow seem to know about bad behaviors in a way that might seem magical or Godlike to unsophisticated, young minds. If you're one of the majority of children who were punished for bad behavior, chances are that you may have some form of "punishment mentality" concept stuffed away in the foundations of your personality and worldview.

When you have punishment mentality, you may think that you don't deserve all the blessings that are your birthright. You know that you've made mistakes, and if God doesn't punish you for them, by golly, you'll have to do it yourself.

Instead of sinking to such depths, we can use our minds to uplift these harmful beliefs into a beneficial belief in a benevolent God. Then, we'll be opening the door to spiritual happiness.

Instead of thinking about your challenges with punishment mentality, you can contemplate them with faith in God's limitless grace. Perhaps you have been given extra challenges because your heart is longing to truly be free, and those troubles are exactly what will get you there. Perhaps you dared to wish for the experience of God's presence in every moment of your life, or for divine grace to inspire and bless your works. Such blessings don't always come cheap or without challenges that may be necessary to test, transform, and uplift you.

> *Here is a test to find whether your mission on earth is finished: If you're alive, it isn't.*
> – Richard Bach

Consider that, through your challenges, God may be rearranging things to loosen your attachments, heal your pride, or prepare the way for some new growth in your deep inner life. Of course, you can also make efforts to lower the number of corrections you have to go through by adjusting your actions. However, contrary to what you may have learned as a child, there is no need to think that a parental God is ready and waiting to punish you if you do something wrong. This is where the idea of God as a benevolent teacher can come in handy.

Many ancient spiritual scriptures explain that *we* create the world as we live it — each one of us, and all together. Therefore, we can choose to create the experience of a loving God, or we can create the experience of a judgmental, harsh, and wrathful God who sends afflictions to express his displeasure with something we've done. The seeds of spiritual happiness or unhappiness exist in how we interpret the events of our lives.

Even if we don't always have a choice over how outer events and experiences take place, we do have some say as to how we interpret those situations. In fact, we can even learn to be grateful for challenges when our focus is on how to use them as leverage to improve ourselves.

CB

Things Don't Have to Be So Hard

The good, the bad, hardship, the joy, the tragedy, love and happiness are all interwoven into one single, indescribable whole that is called life.
–Jacqueline Kennedy

Many spiritual books, including this one, tell us that we should learn to grow from our pain and to bear all the obstacles of life with faith in the ultimate goodness and perfection of this universe. However, it is important to realize that we can grow, not only through hardship, but also through joy.

One of the main secrets of spiritual happiness is that things don't have to be so hard. Spirituality doesn't have to be so hard. Life doesn't have to be so hard. Learning our lessons doesn't have to be so hard. Some people always seem to look at life through the glasses of "everything is hard," and you can be sure that such glasses are bound to affect their experience of happiness and unhappiness.

One fairly advanced level of spiritual growth is to learn to be happy even during trials and tribulations. However, even if we're not always able to stay perfectly happy during bad times, we can at least learn to be happy when things are going well! I know people who have great blessings in their lives, but who complain about being depressed and appear to be much more upset about their few challenges than grateful for their massive blessings.

Some people even find that they are actually *happier* during tough times, because their appreciation for small and large blessings becomes more sensitized and awakened. Challenges may require us to drop our layers of superficial boredom and dissatisfaction and to draw upon inner resources of strength, fortitude, courage, gratitude, wisdom, prayer, and a positive mindset.

If we can't be happy even when things are going well, then what option does our kind and loving destiny have but to try another approach and shake us into gratitude and happiness through trauma?

In fact, troubles and strife can become somewhat of a habit for some folks. They can give a rush of mental energy, and a stimulus of emotions, and therefore, these catastrophe rushes can actually become addictive habits. Don't you know some people who seem to just land in one tragedy after the other? I've seen some like this, and it's almost like God is using these tragedies as a medicine to shake them into wakefulness, or to help them to feel more alive.

Nevertheless, with spiritual practices and wisdom, we can learn to create the same kind of excitement, enthusiasm, and growth inside ourselves without having to go through so many hard times.

Remember, sometimes life is hard, and sometimes life is not so hard. When it is not so hard, don't make it hard!

Open Yourself to Inner Guidance

Sometimes, we think we're supposed to fix everything in our lives, and maybe we're really only supposed to learn something from the situation.
– Louise Hay

One helpful secret of spiritual happiness is to learn how to teach, guide, and lecture yourself. Don't always wait for someone else to lecture you. Don't think that you have to keep buying books, going to workshops, and seeking knowledge from others. That's all fine, but you can also learn to find wisdom and guidance inside yourself.

Even our choices of outer knowledge can be motivated by inner guidance. If we do want to enjoy a lot of outer classes, workshops, audio books, and other sources of external wisdom, we can still allow our *inner guidance* to help us choose from where we will receive our *outer guidance*.

Once you realize that a great wise soul exists inside of you, you'll be able to seek answers within your own depths of wisdom. If you have made a mistake, you'll be able to contemplate and learn from what you did. You don't have to chew your head off or criticize yourself into the ground when something goes wrong. Be honest and loving with yourself. Guide yourself, and invite your wise and compassionate soul to have a stronger voice within your being.

Our recognition and acknowledgement of the inner wisdom is a kind of invitation for it to speak more clearly. Actually, the inner guide is always speaking – the universal soul exists inside each one of us, and speaks to and through everybody. Our job is to learn how to listen to that pure note above the cacophony of not-so-wise thoughts and sounds.

Inside yourself, invite your own wise soul, your own bit of divinity, to speak to you. You can also ask for guidance from your own clear intelligence, or even from your knowledgeable subconscious mind, which has access to all kinds of information that your conscious mind doesn't. Open to whatever within yourself is greater than the usual realm of hashed and rehashed superficial experiences and thoughts. Turn your attention inside, and let your inner wisdom guide you and give you advice.

You know more than you live; we all know more than we live. I know a lot more than I live, but I have also tended to seek guidance within and to lecture myself from within. And in my books, I lecture myself, and *you* get to listen in.

If you're feeling upset about something, take time to talk within your mind. Even while talking with others about whatever events may be sparking your feeling of upset, use those discussions to explore your own thoughts, and to gather advice and information that may help you more effectively figure things out and heal your troubles. Don't just share your woes over and over without purpose, because the more you repeat your troubles, the stronger they are likely to become. Remember how powerful your words and thoughts are, and with that remembrance, seek guidance within yourself.

If you're feeling unhappy or upset, remind yourself of what you know, what you've read, what you've learned, and what you've thought during happier times. If this doesn't come easily, try picking up some uplifting spiritual writings to see if they'll spark your inner wisdom. Then, enter your deeper knowledge that exists even beyond what you've read, learned, and thought. Trust God, trust the universe, trust your own great Self, and open up to your inner guidance.

Teaching, guiding, or lecturing yourself doesn't mean that you put yourself down any kind of demeaning or judgmental way. Guide yourself lovingly. Talk to yourself with kindness. If you're feeling angry, lecture yourself as though you were your best friend, trying to help you to get through this anger.

If you're feeling sorrowful, ask your inner wise soul to remind you that grace can work through a broken heart to create an even greater space for joy, and to teach us to have greater surrender, humility, or compassion. While respecting whatever emotions you are feeling, remind yourself to always have faith. Talk to yourself about what you truly believe, and remind yourself of the great wisdom that you already know. This is what many spiritual sages refer to when they say that you

154

are ultimately your own guru. In this view, a good outer guru exists to guide you into a stronger relationship with the universal guru or guide who exists everywhere, including right inside of you.

Guide yourself. Contemplate deeper meanings behind the experiences of life. Give yourself challenges and disciplines that will help to refine and uplift you. Figure out what is causing you problems in your life, and open your mind and heart to the guidance of inner wisdom and intuition. Ask yourself how you can resolve or transform those troubling causes. Discern whether to best heal those problems with an internal shift of attitude, or through external actions, or both. Help yourself, guide yourself, and be your own best friend, always. This is a great path to spiritual happiness.

C3

Do What Your Heart Knows is Right

Happiness is the reward we get for living to the highest right we know.
–Richard Bach

An important secret of spiritual happiness is to always strive to do what you believe in your heart to be good and right.
Doing what you really believe is good and right automatically brings more spiritual happiness. The more you can live in a way that is consistent with what you believe is right, the more peace you will enjoy. You won't be walking around, plagued by nagging pains about all the ways that you may have violated your own morals. You won't be weighed down by mountains of guilt, shame, and disappointments.

If you go against what you know is right, you may sometimes create a semblance of temporary outer happiness – such as by gaining some material benefit from pulling one over on someone else, or from thinking that you're better than someone else, or while laughing about having put somebody down. However, if you know deep inside that you have violated one of the important laws of goodness and decency, then your long-term spiritual happiness will become diminished and depleted, even if your outer happiness has temporarily increased.

Let's say that you've managed to acquire a whole bunch of money by ripping people off. You get to buy a big, brand-new house and expensive new cars. Your whole life has apparently improved, and you appear to be happy, happy, and happy. But, perhaps, your spiritual happiness is not so good. And truthfully, if your spiritual happiness is not so good, then that will eventually erode even the outer happiness. Either you will lose what you had, or you'll become dissatisfied regardless of everything you have. Eventually, you'll no longer be happy – inwardly, outwardly, relatively or spiritually. Nothing will be enough to fill the black hole of emptiness that comes from harming somebody else to benefit yourself. Your soul knows better.

On the other hand, if you go out of your way to be righteous and kind, and in the process end up with outer lacks that cause a certain amount of outer unhappiness, then your righteousness and kindness may still bring you greater spiritual happiness, in spite of the outer challenges.

Even when things appear to be going wrong in our lives, we can maintain a connection with spiritual happiness just by living according to our highest morals and aspirations. As spiritual happiness shines from within our hearts, amazing miracles may also take place in our outer lives, eventually creating more happiness all the way around. Therefore, if you had to choose between outer happiness and spiritual happiness, my suggestion would be to choose spiritual happiness.

Spiritual happiness comes from acting in accordance with our deepest knowledge and wisdom about what is good, what is true, and what is right. Somebody who becomes apparently happy by taking advantage of others may think that he or she is happy, but deep in their soul, there is not the kind of happiness that will remain throughout their life, or at the moment of their death. On the other hand, righteous living and spiritual happiness are beloved friends during our lives, and continue to give us great comfort and support when the time comes for us to leave this world.

Obviously, each of us is fallible as we walk through the path of life, so there is no need to berate yourself for falling short of your greatest aspirations and ideals. Just keep striving to do what you know in your heart is right, and to continue to learn and grow from your mistakes. Listen to the inner guide who tells you when you've done something wrong, as clearly as the dramatic music in a movie would tell you that something bad just happened. You can also learn to hear that music inside of you – a dramatic feeling, announcing that you've created something you don't want by doing something you know isn't right.

The more attuned we become to hearing, seeing, thinking, or feeling this *nudging nag* from our inner selves, the sooner we can change our mode of action to be in greater harmony with what we know is right – and the sooner we get to bask in the golden rays of spiritual happiness.

಼

Uplift Your Motives

What is the best way to go beyond self-interest and obsession with personal demands, needs and disappointments? The answer is: Whatever you do, may it benefit everyone.
– Gurumayi Chidvilasananda

Let's be honest. Anytime anyone does anything, it is for a reason, and with a motive. Even if you are the most altruistic person in the world, selflessly helping people wherever you go, there is still some subtle motive. Perhaps it is the motive of feeling good about yourself, or of pleasing God, or creating good *karmas* or merits for your future. There are millions of possible motive configurations. Each person carries within themselves a unique mixture of pure and impure motives.

Once we've recognized that our actions are ultimately motive-based, then, instead of always struggling to rein in our outer behavior, we can focus more of our efforts on improving our knowledge, understanding, and spiritual vision in ways that will uplift our motives, thereby naturally purifying and clarifying our actions.

For some, their primary motives may be as simplistic as materialistic greed or a desire for power over others. We all know how that kind of movie eventually ends. Others may be motivated by a wish to have as good a time as possible, without harming others. Still others may dedicate their lives to serving humanity, and will receive a sense of fulfillment from that. Then you have the extremes of Buddhist Bodhisattvas, some of whom take vows to keep reincarnating into human form until every single other soul has reached enlightenment and freedom from the cycles of birth and death.

Most of us are somewhere in-between the corrupt and greedy executives who have wrecked their companies, resulting in misery for many innocent investors who lost their life savings, and the saintly Bodhisattvas who vow to uplift every soul and stay to clean up after the whole "party" ends.

Just notice and observe where you are on the mixed-motivations chart. As you go through your day and through the events of your life, pay attention to what is motivating you to do whatever you are doing. Why are you extra nice to certain people, and perhaps less so to others? Why are you more generous in some situations than in others? Is your inner satisfaction from doing good enough to keep you doing good, or does there have to be some obvious payoff?

One great step we can take toward purifying our motives is to look for ways to help those who would apparently never be in a position to return the favor. Through this kind of selfless giving, we get to relish the pure and naked joy of being helpful. We learn to be a willing instrument of God's grace upon this earth.

> *The best index to a person's character is (a) how he treats people who can't do him any good, and (b) how he treats people who can't fight back.*
> — **Abigail van Buren ("Dear Abby")**

Then you have the *Siddhas*. These are rare beings who have transcended common motivations. After attaining an enlightened view of life, they realized that there was no separate "I," and therefore no reason for worldly motivations. Some of these beings have appeared to be strange or mad, but those who really got to know these Siddhas would find them to be filled with spiritual wisdom, and to be great bestowers of grace.

One Siddha, named Hari Giri Baba, used to wear a big overcoat. Hari Giri Baba would fill his pockets with stones as he walked along the road. He would enthusiastically pull out a stone and show it to someone, saying, "This is worth ten thousand rupees!" You have to admit that this is a good example of having reverence for even a stone in God's divine creation.

Many stories have been told of those who were healed of major ailments after receiving one of Hari Giri Baba's stones. Hari Giri Baba was highly respected for his great wisdom and ability to bestow blessings, and today there is even a temple in India that is dedicated to Hari Giri Baba.

There is also a temple dedicated to another Siddha, Zipruanna, who would sit naked on a big pile of garbage, yet who was said to have always exuded a sweet fragrance, in spite of his immediate environment.

This type of drastic detachment is a possible "side-effect" that could potentially come about if we were to become totally and completely free from all motivations. But, don't worry, it is a rare accomplishment. If any of us should be fortunate enough to become completely free of any self-interest or tainted motivations, it would probably feel just fine to sit anywhere at all. Zipruanna was also an ecstatic being who also had many powers, such as those that we would call psychic abilities.

Here's an example of how someone who is free from motivation leaves this world:

One day Zipruanna knocked on the door of a family who lived in the village where he sat on his garbage pile "couch." In spite of his external appearance, the townsfolk considered Zipruanna to be a great and wise sage, and this family was only too happy to invite him in. Zipruanna asked to take a rare bath, and then requested some rice and vegetables. After completing his meal, Zipruanna said, "Zipru is leaving. You can cry now," and closed his eyes. He was gone.

> *Those who are desireless have no fear; those who are desireless are always happy.*
> – **Bhagavan Nityananda**

Now, you don't have to go to such extremes in trying to purge yourself of all motivations. Just pay attention to your motives, and look for ways to uplift and purify them. See if you can find happiness just from doing something well, or from finding ways to give happiness to others. Find your own methods for uplifting your motives.

Make efforts to enjoy doing what you know is right just because you know it is right, and not only so you can acquire more material goods for doing it. See if you can enjoy doing something well without even taking or receiving credit for doing it.

When we act from an enjoyment of doing what is right in each moment, then our actions have a shimmer of purity and truth to them, regardless of what those specific actions are. It is a matter of keeping a greater intention while acting – an intention that blesses you, me, and the whole world. Let's act in ways that honor ourselves and others. Let our motivations come from a strength of spirit that is free from the lower-energy pulls of greed and other impure desires.

With purified motives, life's inevitable disappointments also tend to have less sting. After all, without a lot of motives, you can't really be too easily disappointed. You'll tend to accept and welcome whatever comes with a more positive attitude. You may continue to work enthusiastically toward your goals, but with an underlying sense of surrender to "Thy will be done."

With the spiritual awareness of "Thy will be done," all news becomes good news – whether it is news of loss or gain. *Thy Will Be Done* can never lose, because the Divine Will is always Done. It is eternal, all-pervasive, all-knowing, all-powerful, and always perfectly contented and in harmony with everything, large or small, that exists in this entire creation. Thy Will Be Done is an inherently winning hand, and a great hand up to the summit of spiritual happiness.

Trust the Perfection in Imperfection

The true work of art is but a shadow of the divine perfection.
– Michelangelo

One concept that has been especially helpful to me on my journey of spiritual happiness is the idea that everything is always perfect – that this whole universe is perfect in a profoundly ultimate sense. One

Hindi poem says that not even a leaf moves without God's will. Another poet declared that God can even hear the footsteps of an ant – imagine that! The idea behind these images is that God is all-perfect and all-knowing, and that this universe is God's creation.

The awareness of universal perfection within the appearance of imperfection is a magical key to faith, and faith is a magical key to spiritual happiness.

It is easy to accept that anything that has taken form in this world is inherently imperfect, including people and institutions. This is obvious from watching the doings of everyone from large corporations, to world politicians, to celebrities, to just about every kind of person who has lived on this earth. Imperfection is quite obvious in this world. However, what allows us to be spiritually happy, even in the face of worldly imperfection, is to open our eyes, minds, and hearts to discerning and accepting the idea of universal perfection. A vision of universal perfection allows us to relax into the deepest levels of our spiritual selves.

Just watch nature taking her disciplined courses of events, with seasons arising and subsiding with great steadiness (aside from a few ice ages and a bit of global warming here and there.) With our newest telescopes, we can see galaxies and universes being created and destroyed in grand dances of massive beauty. On this magnificent planet earth, oceans stay in their place, mountains remain firm, and animals of every species are born equipped with just the right instinctual knowledge to take care of themselves and their young. These are just a few hints of what universal perfection looks like in action.

On one hand, we must accept the imperfection of this world. This is important, because it keeps us from having unrealistic expectations that would become broken again and again, thus bringing unhappiness. With an acceptance of the imperfect nature of this world, we can actually attain more peace, contentment, and happiness, because we are no longer having our expectations broken and disappointed at every turn.

At the same time, we can trust in an ultimate perfection beyond the grasp of the limited structures and abilities of our minds. We can trust that, in some way, this entire creation simply *must* be perfect, even if it doesn't always appear so to our limited minds. This trust is a porthole into a different kind of knowing that brings faith, optimism, and hope to support and maintain our spiritual happiness.

Eventually, steeped in the vision of universal perfection, we swim in the faith and trust that everything in every moment is absolutely perfect, destined, and meant to be. Even while making efforts in the world, we rest in knowing that only the great universal power acts through us. No blame, no shame, no gain, no pain — just universal perfection dancing in front of us, around us, and inside of us, as us. It's not that everything has to always look perfect for us to choose to trust this perfection. Nor does it mean we wouldn't continue to make efforts to improve ourselves.

The awareness of perfection in imperfection is an inner knowing, an inner trust, and a soothing place of inner rest. We all know this perfection deep inside, because we are all one with the universal flow of perfection deep inside. It is like a thread, and we are all like beads on that one thread. Everything in this whole magnificent universe – from the tiniest revolving electrons to massive exploding galaxies – is strung on this thread of universal perfection. When you know that you too are an integral element of this amazing dance of universal perfection, then spiritual happiness is in your hand – and *you* are in the hand of spiritual happiness.

CB

See the Bigger Picture of
Your Soul's Journey

*Man's unhappiness.... comes of his greatness; it is
because there is an Infinite in him, which, with all his
cunning, he cannot quite bury under the finite.*
—*Thomas Carlyle*

We are so much more than we can ever know. One great key to
spiritual happiness lies in our choice of identification.

Each of us is a spark of the eternal, great, soul that exists beyond time
— the "Before Abraham was, I Am" aspect of all creation. Yet, we are
also people who apparently exist in time and space, with all that
entails. The entire spiritual journey takes place between these two
aspects of ourselves — the little petty guy who is concerned about
many things that are not so important in the grand scheme of things,
and the eternal, great soul who is the *source* of the whole grand scheme
of things. And what a journey it is!

In the grand scheme of things, our individual life is like being on a
vacation, though admittedly, not always the most pleasant one. But
haven't you ever been on a vacation gone bad? It happens. Recently
in the news, many people have been going on cruises where hundreds
of the guests ended up quite ill — a good example of vacations gone
bad. Of course, life is a bigger journey than just a weeklong cruise;
therefore we have many more opportunities for all kinds of experiences — good, bad, pleasant, and unpleasant.

At the end of this "life-vacation," our deepest soul also gets to go home
— wherever that unknowable home may be. In fact, some say that our
deepest soul has never left home, and that all the colorful phantasma-

goria of life is but a dream in the mind of God, the Supreme Soul who "dreams" us all into existence.

If we identify only with the *little us* – who goes by our name and has all of our limited and individual personality and physical traits – then we are likely to experience the ups and downs of life as huge waves that may engulf us. All the troubles in life become so big and important. We ride the not-so-thrilling roller coaster of happy and sad, which never truly comes to rest in the depths of true spiritual happiness.

If, instead, we identify with our unknowable greatness, through knowledge, contemplation, and faith, then we become spectators of our own life. As spectators, we can enjoy the show, regardless of whether it is appearing as a drama, a comedy, or perhaps even a tragedy. We naturally see the inherent beauty and perfection of life. The key is to look at life as a play and to enjoy the show!

Now, with this expanded view in mind, I'd like to be your tour guide on a little side trip of this journey. I'm going to share with you a visualization and contemplation exercise that can be used to symbolically dissolve any situation that is troubling you or holding you down at this particular time in your life. Image-based contemplations like this can help us to get over inner stresses, such as anger, fear, grief, and all the other emotions that create obstacles in our lives and block our experience of spiritual happiness.

Choose your most potent trouble – whether it's a big worry that is shadowing you, a contentious situation you may have with someone at work, an inability to forget or forgive someone who you feel has harmed you, or a major loss that you may have recently suffered. If you can't find anything from recent years, well, bully for you. You can go back as far as needed to find an appropriate problem. If there aren't any, even from childhood, then you're either dead or enlightened, and why are you reading this book?

Don't just choose the situation, but really get into all the emotions you have about the matter. If it's a memory that brings up anger, bring forth the anger fully. If it's something you've complained and moaned about to friends, then bring up all those angry words you've said out loud and in your mind. Really get into the feeling, down to its roots – which may even be in childhood experiences that you don't consciously remember.

Whatever the charged feeling is, elicit it. Feel it. Make the problem as big in your mind as it has ever been. Don't judge what you feel, or limit what you feel. Just take a moment to close your eyes and jump into the fire of whatever is most bugging you in life right now. Don't worry, this book won't burst into flames, and the pages can also withstand a few tears, should they come forth.

How are you doing? Sorry if I've bummed you out a bit, but don't worry, it's for a good cause – clearing the way for your long-term happiness.

Now take all that big mass of negativity that you've invoked, and with your mind's eye and your heart's intention, bring it all together into a big ball. Imagine your hands bringing the whole troubling situation, along with all the energies and emotions that come with it, together into a big ball. With your mind's imagination, pack all the troubles together tightly, as you might pack together a snowball.

Now imagine that the background of your field of vision is the physical universe – a black tapestry with many specks of colored and white lights, spinning, smashing, and flickering. Your hand appears as a big cosmic hand made of glittering blue star stuff, and the ball of negativity is also made of the same shimmering stardust. Bring your ball into center stage.

Hold it and look at it – this fiery blue ball of energy spinning in your cosmic stardust hand, this problem that has been bugging you.

This ball is not made of solid stuff, but of a combination of words, thoughts, perceptions, emotions and experiences – just as the planet Saturn is not solid, but is rather a round mass of gas particles that have coalesced together. The particles that have coalesced into your ball of troubles are made of all the images and thoughts that you've had regarding the challenging situation. Ultimately, even these are made of the same shimmering spiritual essence that creates the best of times, the worst of times, and all times.

Many scientists, spiritual sages, and philosophers of various traditions would agree on one thing: everything that exists anywhere, in any way, is ultimately made up of nothing but energy, solidified light. All that exists is a manifestation of pure spirit, supreme consciousness, and cosmic creative awareness. The whole shebang emanates from the very Mind of God that thinks you and me into existence, breathing amazing life into, through, and *as* each one of us.

With this elevated viewpoint, look at the ball of troubles spinning in your shimmering cosmic hand, amidst the spotted blackness of space. It's right there in your hand – the whole situation that has been causing you so much trouble, whether for the past few weeks, or the past 50 years, or from even beyond what you are aware of as your current life.

Look out into the seemingly infinite expanse of space around you. This universe is so big. Enjoy being a speck of divine life in the midst of this vast blanket of physical existence. From this vantage point, the problem probably doesn't look quite so big and insurmountable, does it? From this expanded perspective, feel and affirm your power to uplift and transform the problem, from the soul-roots out.

You don't necessarily have to go through decades of psychotherapy, unraveling the memories of every past trauma, in order to find the roots of your present woes. Just invoke all the known and unknown elements that make up this apparent problem with the power of your will. Now, with the authority of the spheres, declare the problem to be healed, and no longer a problem.

With a spiritual awareness of this universe as a creation of the one, eternal, and all-pervasive creative being, you'll have an ability to heal problems from the inside-out, instead of only from the outside-in. You'll be able to address problems on the much more effective soul level.

When you try to heal something from the outside-in, things can get very complicated, because you're working with so many varied layers in the outer world of appearances. However, when you heal a problem on the soul level, all the outer distortions that have come from that problem begin to "magically" disappear and heal.

Solving problems on the outer level alone becomes somewhat of a hit and miss game. Which knob can you turn to solve a problem? What thoughts can you think to stop worrying about a problem? With outer efforts alone, you can spend a great deal of time searching and researching, and still come out with "ring around the collar" – or troubles in your bubbles.

If, instead, you can raise your personal awareness into your greater, universal self, then you have much more ability to direct the play of your life through your power of intention. That is what we are doing with this visualization exercise – elevating our awareness so that we can heal this problem through the powerful intention of our stronger link – our expanded, creative, harmonious, universal link.

Look again at the problem in your great cosmic hand, and know that you can choose to let go of it right now, just by clearly choosing to let it go. The key is to make your choice unanimous throughout your being – without holding on to the problem situation for whatever side benefits your weaker self may think it is deriving from these negative emotions and thoughts.

There are many reasons why we may hold on to problems in life – perhaps using sadness or setbacks as excuses for lethargy or mediocrity, or using anger or worry to support a habit of emotional energy bursts, or to score some positive attention or care from others.

Other reasons for choosing to persevere through troubles may be more positive and spiritual. Maybe you would choose to stay in an uncomfortable relationship because you know that this is the only way for your soul to release old negative patterns, or to learn how to have more patience, or to uncover your ability to give and love unconditionally. Maybe you've accepted a time of poverty because you can sense that this challenge is helping you learn how to have greater faith in God's compassionate presence and protection on a day-to-day and minute-by-minute basis. Troubles can certainly be good inspirations in reminding us to pray, and pray sincerely!

As you hold this ball of troubles in your hand, see if it holds any benefits that you may wish to keep for yourself. Even just this one step of acknowledging any possible benefits you may be receiving from a set of troubles brings you back into the driver's seat of your life. You enter back into the realm of choice, the fountainhead of life that creates and recreates everything in every moment.

Now, take the ball of unwanted feelings and situations that you are holding it in your imagined cosmic hand. Shake the ball of troubles, waving it around enthusiastically until all the particles fly off and become more shimmering stardust streaming through endless, deep, dark space. Smile and wave at the radiant, lustrous particles that once were your resentment, fears, frustrations, angers, and disappointments. Goodbye! Don't come again!

Watch as all the blue shimmering particles of that circumstance fly freely, dissolving from the ball, and dancing through the tapestry of universal space. Now, pick up a big cosmic broom, and cheerfully sweep it all away, sprinkling glittering blue light stardust all over, to the farthest reaches of space, as all the particles settle back into the ground from which all creation comes forth. Appreciate the underlying beauty that existed even in that challenging circumstance, and thank God for giving and now removing the problem.

As other troubles or challenges arise in your journey of life, you can also see them as sparkling particles of divine consciousness, and offer them back into their universal source.

See the bigger picture of your soul's journey, and be free. Herein lies the essence of spiritual happiness.

☙

Enjoy the Trip!

If your daily life seems poor, do not blame it; blame yourself, tell yourself that you are not poet enough to call forth its riches.
– **Rainer Maria Rilke**

Let's revisit the idea that, in the eternally big scheme of things, this whole life journey is like going on vacation for a few weeks. During the vacation, various events take place — some things go the way we've planned, and some things don't go the way we've planned. During and after this trip, *we* are the one who have a choice of what to focus on, and how we want to experience and remember the time. Do we focus on the good aspects of the trip, or do we complain about things that didn't turn out the way we wanted them to?

This is an important question; because one of the most important secrets is that our attention is the key to our spiritual happiness. Whatever we focus our attention on grows – it's as though we are watering ideas and situations like plants, with the waters of our powerful thoughts. Therefore, the more we focus on positive, happy thoughts, the more we'll be invoking greater happiness in our lives.

Upon returning from a vacation, when you talk about the trip, would you tend to focus mostly on complaining about the challenges – the fact that maybe the airlines lost your luggage for a while, or the hotel room reservations had gotten mixed up? Or would you focus on all the great experiences you had — all the interesting people you met, all the new cultures you discovered, all the great purchases you made, and the many other positive aspects of your journey?

Now, I'm not suggesting that we should be dishonest or pretend that bad things never happened. Obviously, if challenges happened, they happened, and can be considered as parts of a well-rounded vacation. We can still include challenges in a well-rounded assessment of our life journey, and we can include them in a positive way.

One way to turn almost any challenging situation into a positive one is through the magical elixir of humor. Humor will definitely help to make our journey more happy and fun, so laugh away. Laugh at the triumphs and the tribulations. Laugh at your greatness and your imperfections. Laugh at the cosmic joke that runs, like a stream, alongside the ever-flowing waters of spiritual happiness.

You know, troubles can be pretty funny if they're experienced and told with an awareness of the cosmic joke. If you just report back that, "Oh, we went here for a vacation, and everything was perfect," that may be a little boring for your audience. And remember that God is also always your audience!

However, challenges or unforeseen mix-ups during your journey can lead the way to having more entertaining stories to tell. In many ways, spiritual happiness is all about being a good storyteller – even just in how you look at the events of life in your own mind.

I learned this lesson while writing my first book, which happened to be an autobiography. What an amazing process it was to look back at my whole life, from infancy on, and to choose what to share with the world. During this process, I also realized that some of my most precious possessions were my stories. Good, bad, ecstatic, or shocking — if it was a good story, it was a gem in my treasure house of life.

While going through a whole lifetime of events, I realized that I could write my life as the saddest story you could imagine, or as the most blessed one — and it was all in the interpretation, and in which aspects of an experience I chose to highlight.

In fact, I can also tell quite a bit about readers by how they interpret and respond to my stories. Some have said, "You have lived the greatest life!" while others have said how sorry they felt for all the challenges I had to go through. Some laugh, some cry, and most laugh and cry together. Some thanked me for writing a powerful and intimate tribute to the spiritual path I described in the autobiography, while one woman actually attacked and accused me of trying to destroy our spiritual path and our guru by sharing my stories so honestly. I began to see that the stories of life are like mirrors, and that each listener's own image is reflected in how they view, interpret, and respond to whatever they hear, see, or read. Of course, this experience also helped me to pay more attention to when I was projecting my own deep-seated attitudes or feelings onto my interpretations of others.

While writing my stories, I also moved beyond judging specific incidents as simply "good" or "bad." I began to see the events of my life as an artist might look upon whatever they encounter. If it was a good story that brought personal growth and lessons, then it was good, regardless of whether the experience was pleasant or not.
I remembered that to an artist, even an overflowing garbage can in the alley could have great beauty. An artist might even want to paint the scene – with all the glistening reflections of the rising sun falling upon the garbage can and the wrappers, papers, and bottles that have overflowed onto the ground.

I decided to live life as a spiritual artist – greeting whatever I see with a reverence and appreciation for its hidden or manifest beauty. I decided to enjoy the trip. Not only did I learn to look at the past events of my life with an artist's perspective, but I was also able to bring that same artist's point of view with me into the present moment. After writing my life story, I began to see all the challenges I was continuing to go through as even more good stories. I'd see the story and the challenges, but the story first. Even when I was sad or suffering in the midst of various outer troubles, a part of me was taking notes and enjoying the show, while striving to discover and reveal the blessings and lessons inherent in each particular configuration of life experience.

Another great tool that has helped me to enjoy my trip has been to do what any good tourist would do – take pictures! If you are able to, I'd suggest purchasing a camera and seeking out beauty to capture with it. This is a great method for training yourself to look for beauty and to develop an artist's eye for God's grand creation. Technology has now moved forward to the point where you can even find digital cameras that never require additional costs of film or developing. You can just snap away, upload the good photos to a computer, and erase the memory card to reshoot some more.

❧

Be Optimistic

I intend to live forever—so far, so good.
– Stephen Wright

Possibly the number one secret of spiritual happiness is to be an optimist. Once you've attained true optimism, you will be spiritually happy, because you'll have absolute trust and faith. Optimism ultimately boils down to an absolute trust that everything is always, ultimately fine.

One way to create optimism is by interpreting events and circumstances through a positive worldview. This doesn't mean that we'll always to be able to come up with every possible positive explanation for each event in our lives. After all, every point of energy in this massive universe is a universe in and of itself. Life is big, big, big — as the ancient scriptures say, bigger than the biggest.

Nevertheless, we can start by asking questions such as, "Why might this event have happened to me, and what shift did it create in my world?" "Why might I have lost this thing or gained another?" Just as we may have contemplated certain symbolic interpretations of our sleeptime dreams, in the same way, we can also learn to interpret the rich symbolism and brilliance that is inherent in our daily life. And, just as each object in our dreams may have several symbolic interpretations, in the same way, in our "waking life dream," many symbolic interpretations are also possible for the events and objects in our lives.

Optimism means to choose interpretations that lead to positive thoughts. For example, I've found the idea of *detoxing* to come in handy when I get a cold. Even while acknowledging the outer circumstances or habits that may have contributed to the cold, I'll usually visualize the cold helping my body to clear out some old, unhelpful residue of one thing or another from my body. I may assume that the fever, sneezing, coughing, and other symptoms are doing just that. This way, I am sending my own good energy intentions into the situation, along with a positive image of detoxing and healing.

Even while watching the leaders of my country sometimes pursue certain actions that I've disagreed with, I've also continued to visualize a positive result from those actions. I believe that a world filled with optimistic well-wishers can heal even large mistakes and create positive results from even questionable actions.

In life, certain outer events may feel terrible and traumatic, and we may experience anxiety about all that is going on during those times. However, if we can possibly rise into the spiritual realm, and also see those painful events from the realm of optimistic faith, then, along with the trauma and the grief of what we've experienced, we may also find a peaceful resting place amidst the storms of worldly tragedy. We'll enter the great and loving shelter of spiritual happiness that exists within and beyond the world of events and appearances.

Poke holes of optimism and faith through the veils of fear and illusion. Shift into a different way of viewing the world. Even though you may not have some of the worldly security nets that you might like, there's nevertheless a higher security — a whole, bigger security that is beyond the worries of this material world. With this kind of faith and optimism, no matter what happens on the worldly level, your soul can remain resplendent and fulfilled in meaningful and powerful ways.

We all have challenging circumstances to go through in life, and we all have unrealized potentials and dreams to realize and achieve. Use the power of optimism to remain anchored in spiritual happiness no matter what. Find something positive in anything and in everything. Seek and realize the goodness in life. Allow your deepest aspirations to blossom forth, regardless of whether they are growing in a clear, pristine lake or in a muddy swamp. Trust that your challenges are coming to you for a blessed reason, and see if you can figure out some of what that reason may be.

> *A pessimist sees the difficulty in every opportunity; an optimist sees the opportunity in every difficulty.*
> - Sir Winston Churchill

Always remember that everything is good, and let everything always be good. Remember, there will always be more. And when there is no more, there will be something else.

Even if you're complaining about something, know in your heart that it is ultimately good. Maybe you're just enjoying having a chance to learn the lessons that come from that particular scenario. Maybe you needed to have a good complaint session to relieve some stress or some tension, or who knows? Maybe your complaints are even meant to help someone else feel better about *their* life.

How amazing is the grand orchestration of this dance of life that moves through and as every one of us, individually, and as a whole. What a sport! What a play! What a grand and magnificent dance this life is.

Maybe you've had to experience the insensitivity of acquaintances to teach you to be more considerate of other people. Maybe your challenging experiences ultimately increased your awareness of your own actions, and have also increased your appreciation for all the good things you already have. Maybe your disappointments in this world are intended to bring your awareness to something even greater than this world.

Look for positive interpretations of things, and let everything be good. Just announce to yourself that every single thing is automatically and unfailingly good. Train your mind to think and accept that everything is good. Listen to your heart, which knows that everything is good. Then, part of the game is to figure out *why* everything may be good, and to come up with possible interpretations for *how* it is all good.

Nevertheless, even if you can't quite figure out how something can be good, you can still trust that – from an unknowable bigger picture – it must be good. This is the practice of intentional and unconditional optimism.

> *Drink in the joy of every moment.*
> – Ram Tirth

With the awareness of universal perfection, and a faith that covers whatever we don't quite understand or know, we rest in the spiritual happiness that comes with trusting in a benevolent universe. Trust that infinite benevolence in every situation, in every second of every day, in every circumstance, in every scenario, in every interaction, and in every moment of happiness, boredom, clarity, fuzziness, excitement, sorrow, and joy.

Maintain an absolute, unshakable, and incorruptible trust in divine, universal benevolence, and you will drink fully of the refreshing waters of spiritual happiness. You'll swim in the ocean of unearthly bliss. You will be living in heaven right here, even while you live on this earth.

May you be blessed with the shining jewel
of spiritual happiness!

Cold Spring Press

We offer bulk purchases at significant discounts. If you are interested in buying this book in quantity, contact us at the address below for more details.

Cold Spring Press
P.O. Box 284, Cold Spring Harbor, NY 11724
E-mail: Jopenroad@aol.com